Business School faculty with Dean Eric Mundinger and President Gordon Wragg at an alumni event in 1979 (see the alumni on page 89)

Building Business

Building Business

Lori Fournier and Don Wheeler

A History of the Business School at Humber

Published by the Business School at Humber through its Academic Publishing Program.
205 Humber College Boulevard, Toronto, Ontario, Canada, M9W 5L7

National Library of Canada Cataloguing in Publication

Fournier, Lori, 1960-
    Building Business: A History of the Business School at Humber / Lori Fournier, Don Wheeler.

Includes index.
ISBN 0-9734977-0-X

    1. Humber College Institute of Technology & Advanced Learning.
Business School–History. I. Wheeler, Don II. Humber College Institute of Technology & Advanced
Learning. Business School. III. Title.

LE3.H873F68 2004   378.713'541   C2004-901021-2

Layout, design and production by Eye Cue Design. Editorial support by Pamela Tulino and Patricia Meek. Project management by Wanda Buote.

Printed in Canada

Table of Contents

FOREWORD

No history can ever be considered complete, and this history of the Business School at Humber is no exception. As we talked to various members of the staff, past and present, we quickly learned that there are many stories within stories. Following up on each and every one would not only be a daunting task, but, if completed, would yield a manuscript equivalent in bulk to several Toronto-size telephone books. Needless to say, that was not a realistic option. Picking and choosing was difficult.

We also became aware that, as we described the evolution of the Business School, it would be helpful to the reader if there was some consistency in terminology. At the beginning, the Business School was referred to as the Business Division and then in the eighties it was changed to the School of Business. We have, however, referred to it throughout by its current name, the Business School.

Job titles have also changed during the past 35 years. Chairman, Chair, Supervisor, Assistant Chair, Program Coordinator and Senior Program Coordinator have been in vogue at various times. Again for consistency, we have used current job title identification for the various positions whenever these positions were part of the story line.

We wish to acknowledge that this trip into the past was a direct result of the initiative and support of the current Dean of the School, Michael Hatton. He felt very strongly that the strengths evident in the Business School today are directly attributable to the work of students, faculty and administrators in the past, and that these efforts should be recognized. On behalf of all those who participated in the Business School during its first 35 years, we thank you Michael.

A debt of gratitude goes to all those who responded to our requests for interviews. Thanks also go to the staff of the various departments in the College who assisted in helping us retrieve data – the Registrar's Office, the Student Placement Office, the President's Office, the AV/Graphics Department, Corporate Services and, of course, the staff and grads of our very own Business School.

In sifting through the various historical data and stories, the essence of the Business School began to emerge. This essence can easily be summarized as:

a spirit of entrepreneurship

a commitment to teamwork

a dedication to client satisfaction, the student and the employer

As you read through the stories and accomplishments of each of the decades, you will easily discern the School's commitment to an exciting future, one where it will be critical to respond to new challenges and opportunities quickly and effectively in order to retain and enhance the Business School's positioning in post-secondary education. Whether it is the strategic introduction of new programs and courses, developing new partnerships, or expanding the levels and reach, the Business School has from the onset continuously positioned itself to be at the forefront in delivering quality and relevant post- secondary business education to students from across Canada and abroad.

We hope that you enjoy reading through the decades as much as we enjoyed writing about them.

Lori Fournier and Don Wheeler

President's Message

There was a time when Humber College was made up of five academic divisions. In the nineties, we evolved into four major schools and six minor schools. Media has become a school unto itself, health is extremely important because of key societal issues related to the aging population, and we have technology with a subset of IT. But business programming remains a fundamental pillar both in breadth of programming and student enrollment. Business students account for 4,000 of our 13,000 total student enrollment.

Business is critical to our economic future. More people want to study business than any other field. And furthermore, you can't have a great college without a great business school, anymore than you can have a great university without a strong medical school or law school.

We have slowly and surely escalated our Business School to be at the top end of the college system, in terms of academic credibility, innovation, and programming breadth. Comparatively, we have a smaller number of business students than some colleges, but we have a more dynamic array of programs and we attract stronger students.

Humber is number one in Ontario, maybe even in Canada. If Humber's reputation is strong, it helps all the Schools. But at the same time, if Humber's Schools are strong, that's what makes Humber's reputation. And the Business School is a cornerstone to our excellent reputation.

Dr. Robert A. Gordon

Message from **Michael Hatton**, Dean of the Business School

You might say that since its inception in 1967, the Business School at Humber College has been lucky. And if you consider that 99 percent of luck is being prepared for opportunities when they come your way, you'd be right.

One of the hallmarks of the Business School has been its foresight. Since the beginning we've worked hard to predict trends and changes coming to business in order to meet the needs of both employers and students. We've been ready when opportunity knocked.

Fortunately, the right people have been in place at the right time. Today's success is the result of 35 years of effort. First and foremost, Humber's presidents, Gordon Wragg and Robert Gordon, have supported the Business School. They have treated it as a cornerstone of the institution and fed and nurtured it appropriately. That's coupled with almost two thousand full- and part-time faculty over three and a half decades who have brought their business experience and academic training into our classrooms and labs. The result has been debate, discussion, and change. Over the decades we've acquired a market position that has placed Humber College and the Business School in the forefront of college education nationally.

While we're proud of our academic accomplishments, we never forget the society we're here to serve. From the beginning, we've remained steadfastly connected to business and are determined to supply the graduates most needed by the economy of the day. We've reached out to employers, who have generously donated their time and energy to our advisory committees. Without them, the education we provide would be lacking the elements of currency and relevance of which we are so very proud.

I'd be remiss if I didn't acknowledge the thousands upon thousands of students who have come to the Business School over the years. So many have achieved particularly noteworthy accomplishments that we couldn't begin to list them all, but let me say that they've been involved in leading some of the country's biggest industries and they've been integral to significant industry advancements. They've been pioneers and entrepreneurs. And so many of these accomplished individuals point proudly to the Business School at Humber College as the place they had their start, as the place where they learned to love a particular subject, or education itself.

And to think – this is only the beginning. The Business School is on the cutting edge of a new kind of community college. We're leading a school of thought that asserts that education isn't for a day or a year, it's for a lifetime.

A sincere thanks to the faculty, staff and graduates who shared their memories so that we can better understand the present, and better prepare for the future.

Dr. Michael J. Hatton

Building Business

Jim Beatty,
President Gordon Wragg,
and Susan Sanderson

Chapter 1
THE 60s: OPPORTUNITY

Chapter 1 The 60s: Opportunity

I hold that man to be right who is most closely in league with the future.

IBSEN

The sixties were years of opportunity. Organizations were expanding and world markets were increasing. Most significantly, technological changes were creating an increased need for trained professionals. Technicians and technologists, first and second level managers, and skilled technical salespeople were all in demand.

At the time, universities were busy meeting the requirements of research and development while providing much-needed undergraduate and postgraduate professionals. Although provincial institutes of trade existed, they weren't sufficient in size, number, breadth or depth to meet the growing demands this era of technological growth had created. What's more, they weren't positioned to meet the needs of the new technologies.

So the government of the day took action. Bill 153 – an act to amend the Department of Education – was introduced. And on May 21, 1965, the Honorable William Davis rose in the legislature to outline the need for responding to the educational challenges at hand and the need to position the education sector so it could better respond to the forecasted growth created by new technologies.

The Minister quoted statements made by the Premier, the Honorable John P. Roberts, in a major statement to the legislature on February 23, 1965, in support of a new college system.

"The long-term solution to most of our problems obviously lies in the development of education and training and the utilization of all our human resources," quoted Davis. "We must prepare Canadian youth to enter the multitude of highly-skilled jobs available today and the ever greater number which will arise in the future."

Davis announced that the new colleges of applied arts and technology would have many facets, such as: high-level programs in office and distributive occupations at the junior and middle management levels, including courses for small business; general adult education courses; retraining, upgrading and updating courses; service industry courses; and commercial courses (such as junior accounting, data processing, and computer programming).

Prophetically, he also pointed out that, "No able and qualified student should be prevented from going on from a college of applied arts and technology to a university."

The regulation made under the Department of Education Act – Colleges of Applied Arts and Technology – was made and approved on October 7, 1965.

Business faculty member Bev Walden (playing guitar) is seen here among other illustrious professors at the first all-campus staff orientation conference at Lake Couchiching in 1968

The first President's Citizenship Medal was awarded to James N. Beatty, a Business Administration student in 1969.

Jim was elected Student Association President, and in 1972 was appointed to the Board of Governors

Bob Bell, member of the original faculty and later School administrative chair, is seen here with his accounting class

The Business School takes shape

Humber College officially opened on Monday, September 11, 1967. Classes were held at James S. Bell Elementary School, a vacated public school on Lake Shore Boulevard West.

While our first programs were rough around the edges, students happily embraced the college system. Many were from high school, but others came directly from the workforce to take advantage of the post-secondary educational opportunities that weren't available when they graduated from high school.

Their enthusiasm was integral to the evolution of the Business School.

In fact, in 1987, when the college celebrated its 20th anniversary, students from the first three-year Business Administration graduating class proudly wore hats with the words "we were there first"

blazoned across them.

Two members of that class — Jim Beatty and David Murray — went on to become members of Humber's Board of Governors. But back in 1967, they were both fresh from high school.

"There was no place for students like me to go," says Beatty, who today owns and operates a graphic design and printing company. "It was either university or work. A lot of us were too immature for the workplace. We could get jobs pumping gas or waiting tables, but you needed skills to build a career."

"Colleges set out to provide job training skills and focus on employability. That's why many of the people I went to school with were older, they came from the workplace to improve their lives."

In those early days, the entire student body numbered only a few hundred. The size, combined with the attitudes of the day, meant that coming to college was a very different experience than it is today.

"In the late sixties there was a lot of student activism. The climate was pretty open. There were no rules and no procedures. If you had a problem, you could walk into the President's Office and get it resolved."

"In general arts you'd find the more rebellious students. In business, we were pretty straight-laced, so we were at the opposite end of the spectrum."

Another very different aspect of college education of the day was the relationship with faculty. Compared to the carefully defined roles of today, the relationship in the early years can best be described as friendly.

"We played pick-up hockey with the faculty," says Beatty. "We invited them to parties. The relationships were quite strong and because they were just out of business their contacts were very good. The interaction with faculty was

fantastic."

He ran for president of the student association and won by eight votes. With Beatty in a leadership role, students became increasingly involved in management committees within the College. "I worked at getting the students a meaningful voice in how the College was run," says Beatty.

Today Dave Murray is a partner in the consulting firm Cane Able Waters and Associates, a career transition business. Back in 1967, he was one of the first students in the Business School.

"Humber appealed because it was new – and living at home was a necessity," says Murray. "Intimacy was a huge factor for me. I had a problem seeing myself in a lecture hall with 200 people."

"I felt there would be a closer affinity with instructors at college. I liked the idea of being taught by people who

had been there, done that. It was intriguing. A big issue for me was exposure and finding mentors or coaches who could share their experiences with me."

Aside from the type of education offered at the new College, the attitude was very appealing. "From a student perspective it was upbeat. We felt like we were in the same boat. It was a lot of fun. And there was closeness in all directions, relative to classmates, to academics, to administration. [President] Gordon Wragg was right there. It wasn't stuffy or formal — it was interactive and participatory."

"I knew I didn't want to work in a factory. Thanks to Don Wheeler and Jim Brodie, I ended up doing what I'm doing now. If I hadn't gone to Humber I wouldn't have found that route."

Faculty member Jim Brodie was a very influential English barrister with a sharp wit and a quick mind. High-profile industry executives

attended his night school course in employment law and benefits. When one of these executives asked if he had a student who might be interested in a job, he announced it to his full-time students.

"After class he said to me, 'you know, work might do you good,'" says Murray about the start of his career. "He was right."

In November 1968, the North campus was officially opened by Mayor E. A. Horton of Etobicoke and Mayor Jack Moulton of York.

"It was totally modern," says Murray. "After the archaic James S. Bell Public School, it was very impressive. It was architecturally modern and it got bigger and bigger. It was a positive change, like going from high school to university.

HUMBER COLLEGE OF APPLIED ARTS AND TECHNOLOGY

CALENDAR 1967-68

I was proud to be there. It felt like we were there at the beginning of something important."

For Jim Beatty, Student Association President in 1969, the creation of the North campus meant many students had a long trek between campuses. And not all students had cars.

"The student association got involved in buying buses to run between campuses. In those days the North campus was in the middle of farmland – there was no bus transportation at all. You could ride horses after class."

Indeed, one of the most common memories of the early days of the North is the mud. Students and faculty

who had cars often had to search for a dry patch, then wade through muck to get to the building. Fortunately, the campus has come a very long way since those days.

Since Jim Beatty and Dave Murray, many graduating students from business have also served on the Board. And, like Jim Beatty, many business students started by serving a term with the student association.

Faculty makes a mark

Early faculty members came from various business and professional disciplines. On average, they had five

to ten years of practical experience along with university degrees and/or professional certification and designations. Many had management and senior management experience. And many were involved in professional associations in areas that became central to the growth of the Business School, including marketing, human resources (personnel), accounting, manufacturing, and purchasing. Despite the lack of formal teacher training, new faculty members related well to the students. Instinctively, faculty worked with students in what today would be called a mentoring system. They were receptive to student input, which was an early characteristic of Humber's Business School environment. Business faculty came to us with a wide variety of experience. For instance, Bill Pitt was a Canadian canoe champion. Pitt organized an after-class ride in a war canoe for members of the first Business Administration class. Although he selected a

safe course on the Humber River, one of the students fell into a muddy section – a cause for much laughter among classmates. "The faculty were our friends and they were passionate about their subject area and their previous field of employment," says Pat Kelly, a student in the second graduating Business Administration class and now Director of Purchasing at the College. "They expected maximum effort and worked with us in developing our potential." The early successes of those first graduating classes made a mark on business and industry. The number of recruiters looking to Humber's Business School increased significantly each spring. Most importantly, high school graduates not wishing to pursue a university degree had an option. More and more, they saw the college system, and Humber College in particular, as a viable alternative for job and career opportunities.

The original Queensway Campus in South Etobicoke

PART-TIME JOBS

PART-TIME JOBS ON CAMPUS
... apply as soon as possible!

JOBS
AVAILABLE

COMPUT

BUSINESS
ALES

TECHNOLOGY

SCIENCES

SEC. CLERICAL

Chapter 2
THE 70s: GROWTH

Chapter 2   The 70s: Growth

If it weren't for college, there would be thousands who had no opportunities at all.

In a word, the seventies were all about growth. Enthusiasm and energy were the order of the day as faculty and support staff worked far beyond the call of duty to spread the word about this innovative new type of education. Numbers were up significantly each year, yet faculty were ceaseless in the promotion of the Business School because they truly believed in what it had to offer students and the business community.

"The growing up of Humber College was an extremely exciting period of time," says Bev Walden, early faculty member and Assistant Dean in the early seventies. "I recall being called into the President's Office and being asked how much it would cost to increase enrolment by 25 percent. I remember sitting in the backyard all weekend with papers all around me, working on figures."

"When you look back on it and the impact we had in those years, it's astounding. Today there are 13,000 students at Humber and when I started there [in 1968] there were a few hundred. In the seventies I was never in a situation when I wasn't hiring faculty. Everything was growth and change related."

Walden also remembers a very different student population.

"It was the time of flower power. A protest campus formed in the ravine," he says about a gathering place behind the building called the Captain America Campus. "Our student association president was a draft dodger from the States and once,

when William Davis was speaking at the North campus, the stage was taken over by anti-Vietnam protestors." One student held up a sign stating, "Business is killing us."

It was a time for action. But acts of rebellion weren't in character for faculty and staff of the Business School. In fact, in the mid-seventies, when Trudeau's government introduced price and wage control, the labour movement wanted a one-day boycott in opposition to the legislation. Staff and faculty chose not to take part, believing it was unprofessional and unethical to withhold services.

Yet their passionate beliefs were powerful motivators for the School.

"We spent every afternoon we could promoting programs and opportunities. The colleges didn't grow up by themselves — it took legwork. We had to convince the business community to get onboard because if we were to provide education that was

worthwhile it had to be recognized by employers. If you weren't out one or two nights a week with prospective employers, you weren't doing your job."

Although the concept was catching on, it was still new for many students. Before the college system, the only options were university or work. And the majority of students weren't qualified for university then.

"Without this chance for education, where would all these people from high school go? If it weren't for college, there would be thousands who had no opportunities at all," says Walden.

But first, students had to understand the concept – and buy into it.

"We had to go to secondary school career fairs, just to explain what community colleges were – it was a tough road."

It didn't take long before students were only too familiar with the benefits of attending a program in the Business School as opposed to working in a factory or starting in the mailroom of a company with a dream of working their way up.

Enrolment grew quickly. By the mid-seventies there were 10 to 14 new sections of the Business Administration program – with 40 students each – every September. Freshman intake was significant. Soon the Business School at Humber College had the largest group of business students in the province.

"We were the showpiece of the college," Walden says. "Our main office was where the bookstore is now – right off the concourse – so we were in the centre of it all."

He adds, "Not only were we a huge division, we were very economical. With the exception of the Hospitality program, the majority of courses were classroom courses, that didn't require labs or technical equipment."

Premier William Davis addresses faculty and students

Student input is central

In those early days, the academic divisions weren't as independent as their size would make them later in the decade. Faculty members worked and played together for the simple reason that there were so few of them.

"One of the things back then," says Don Wheeler, who served a term as Chair in the seventies and again in the eighties, "was that there was a great deal of collegiality because we were all involved in something new. As I like to say, we all started out in the President's Office [in the late sixties], which was the faculty office at the time. We were all there together – all the faculty from all the different divisions. There was a sense of newness and growth."

The manageable size of the School allowed for a unique relationship with students. At universities, students were sitting in crowded lecture halls. In the Business School they were working with faculty to design curriculum. Student involvement was a key factor in program development in the early seventies.

John Almond, Dean from 1967 to 1972, initiated student involvement in curriculum development. Every class in the School appointed a class representative to meet with the Dean and Chairs to discuss the development of courses. In fact, courses proposed for the final semester of a program were often refined before the course was taught based on student input and direct interaction with the faculty member most likely to teach that course.

"At the beginning the Business Administration program had a final compulsory exam, but the students didn't really think it was helpful," says Wheeler. "They wanted an optional exam that would give them a chance to improve their grades if necessary. We listened to their arguments, discussed the issue amongst ourselves, and decided to implement it."

"At the time the program offered specializations," he says. "But students felt that some specializations were easier than others and they wanted consistency. They suggested that a Business Administration diploma should be the same for everyone. Again, we reviewed it and agreed. We revised specializations so all Business Administration students had to take subjects at the same level of difficulty."

"But we didn't lose the idea of specializations entirely. We built business electives into the program so they could still focus on an area if they wished. Students were very pleased with the change."

"They also brought forward the issue of consistency of teaching. They were concerned about standards. Primarily, they wanted more of an applied approach than an academic one. They wanted to be treated as new employees in an organization. That's because a lot of them had work experience. The old teacher/student relationship wouldn't cut it."

What evolved from that input was a higher degree of real world experience. In every course students were required to do an applied project. For instance, a student might follow a salesperson around for a day, or work in a company to evaluate company morale through research and interviews.

Since students were primarily concerned with practice, the programs began to embody a "training" attitude. The move was in tune with what was happening in the business world, since the management style of the day was changing from an authoritative to a participatory style. Managers believed staff were more productive when involved in the planning and design of their jobs.

This mindset had taken a firm hold by the early seventies and greatly influenced the relationship between faculty and students. By the mid-seventies though, the programs had grown too big for regular meetings with faculty.

One initiative that replaced the meetings was a project undertaken by sixth semester Business Administration students, who took on the task of designing and administering a survey for graduates. Their challenge was to determine which courses were most useful to them in their jobs. The project yielded some surprises for students – such as the realization that the unpopular accounting course was one of the most helpful courses in the curriculum – and it served as a guide for curriculum development.

Business comes to school

One of Dean Almond's priorities was to develop communication links with business and industry. He explored the possibility of an exchange whereby an industry person would be seconded to teach in the Business School for one or two semesters, and in turn a faculty member would be seconded to the company.

Arrangements were made to allow Frank Whittam, a member of C.I.L.'s Work Improvement department, to teach the Theories of Management courses. Although some faculty members expressed interest in being assigned to C.I.L., the timing wasn't right and it never happened.

Nevertheless, Whittam not only fulfilled his assignment, he became a full-time faculty member of the Business School until his retirement from the College in 1988. The practical and current knowledge that he brought helped embed an organizational development approach within certain courses. Students

Class representatives in action

in various programs at the School were exposed to the management of change, problem identification and solving, effective versus efficient leadership styles and an understanding of organizational dynamics.

As part of the course curriculum, students were also required to do an actual field assignment with an organization and complete a preliminary diagnosis based on a problem or concern identified by the company. Organizational development courses were the forerunner to the various management approaches that followed. From the "management by walking around" and "in search of excellence" approaches of the eighties, to the Total Quality Management (TQM) systems of the nineties, and Performance Based Management systems of the 21st century, the organizational development approach of the seventies left graduates well prepared for the many changes and approaches that followed. It was a definite advantage when entering the work force.

A very practical approach to education

The early seventies was a time of growth for many industries. In response, the two-year General Business program (later to become Business Management) was introduced in 1972. Operations Management, Personnel Management and Law Clerk profiles were developed for the new program to meet new industry needs.

Students also had the option of creating their own career profile by combining courses offered within the Business School. The foundation courses of this program were the same as in the three-year Business Administration program.

Not only was the new program a godsend for students who had specific career interests in the emerging fields, it allowed the School to respond to the needs of business in a timely fashion.

"It took two years to develop a new program because the Ministry of Education wanted to be sure there were jobs for graduates," says Wheeler. "Programs were restricted throughout the province so when you wanted to introduce a program you had to show through statistics and projections how many jobs would be available in that field. Doing that meant we couldn't respond as quickly. However, by utilizing the profile approach in the General Business program, our response time was very fast. "

"And for those students in the three-year Business Administration program who were thinking about dropping out, it was a way to get specific training in a shorter time period. It was a win-win for employers and students."

A number of these profiles still exist in different forms. Law Clerk developed into the stand-alone Legal Assistant program, then became the Law Clerk program and is the forerunner of today's four-year Bachelor of Applied Arts in Paralegal Studies degree program.

Personnel was another area that evolved, although it had its start earlier than the General Business program. Since it was a projected growth area, it was decided very early that all business students should take a compulsory personnel course as a way to learn about human rights, supervisory skills and leadership skills. That course was the precursor to the Personnel Management career profile, which led to the hugely successful postgraduate Human Resources Management certificate program.

Our practical approach to education was getting noticed. In the early seventies, Marketing Magazine held a competition for college

Faculty member
J. T. Moyes with his
marketing class,
circa 1970

really good for students' egos and great for experience."

From very early on, we worked hard at keeping students engaged with their studies. While there was much discussion about how to prevent them from dropping out, it was Eric Mundinger, Dean from 1972 to 1981, who initiated a program to prevent it. Called ESPIRIT, Dean Mundinger's program was a way to identify students at risk of dropping out.

"We analyzed data to determine who was most at risk," says Wheeler. "Then the Chairs spoke to the students who we determined might leave. We implemented procedures to help them get off the list. Often, they were simply in the wrong area of study or we found they were spending too much time at part-time jobs. Sometimes it was a case of peer tutoring or working with counselling to develop study skills, or simply helping them develop better time management skills."

students. All contestants were given a case study for which they were to work out a solution to be presented to a panel of industry experts, who would determine the winning strategy.

"Our students won three years in a row," says John Liphardt, Chair from 1972 to 1981 and Dean from 1981 to 1987. "At the time, people were not aware of what a college was. The idea had to be sold and the competition got the awareness level up – it helped build credibility. It was

The program proved to be a success. It decreased the dropout rate and helped the faculty realize that many students simply didn't want to spend three years in a business program, which provided more impetus for the growth of the General Business program.

Extra-curricular activities score big with faculty and students

Nowhere was the faculty relationship with students more apparent than in the arena of sports. An integral part of the Business School, sports helped students maintain interest and motivation. What's more, they reinforced the all-important idea of faculty as coaches.

Students and faculty had many golf outings. Eventually students of the Hotel and Restaurant program (which became the Hospitality program) assisted in the organization of a tournament

under the direction of Dean Mundinger. There was also an intramural hockey team called the Apples, and for third-year students in Business Administration, Friday afternoons were reserved for a game of pick-up hockey with faculty.

Many faculty members were also involved at the varsity level. Dean Mundinger coached the men's and women's golf teams and Bev Walden succeeded him. Faculty member Bob Dobson coached the men's and women's varsity curling teams, and faculty members Bill Pitt and John McColl coached football.

"I was very involved in hockey," says Don Wheeler. "Once I acquired my level three coaching certification, I was asked to coach the women's varsity hockey team. We were very successful. We won league titles three times and the provincial championships once."

Being coach of a women's hockey team in those days was a challenge on social fronts as much as anything else.

"The players and I created the Golden Lipstick award for most chauvinistic reporting and delivered it to a writer on the college newspaper who claimed hockey was too dangerous for women. And we made a writer for a daily newspaper a nominee for insisting on calling the team the Hawkettes." (The varsity name is Hawks.)

One of Wheeler's fondest memories is watching the final game of the famous 1972 Canada/Russia hockey series.

"We managed to hook a television up in the staff lounge. When Henderson scored the winning goal, all of the Business School staff and students were packed into a small room. There wasn't even any wiggle room. What a glorious moment!"

Sports was the incentive for a groundbreaking program to motivate students. Because administration insisted that members of varsity teams be students in good standing, players who were not succeeding

academically were made part of a mentoring program run by business faculty. The one-on-one attention was often just the ticket for athletic students with flagging grades.

But business faculty and administration weren't simply jocks. In the early seventies, John Liphardt, then Chair, and professor Jim Brodie were asked by President Gordon Wragg to develop a Sunday afternoon concert series.

"We promoted it in Etobicoke and brought in first-rate musicians," says Liphardt. "The music was followed by tea and cakes or a buffet dinner. The afternoons were a tremendous success and the series continued for a couple of years. And it was all over and above our regular workload."

Significant connections are made

The Hotel and Restaurant program proved very important to the Business

School. In the early seventies the School opened a chic restaurant as a working lab for students. Called Igor's Dining Room in honour of Igor Sokur, the notable chef who became program coordinator, the restaurant was also a place for faculty and administrators to hone business contacts.

On one occasion, administrators were entertaining executives from Shoppers Drug Mart who were so impressed by the real-life lab they were eating in, they decided to hire Business Administration graduates rather than university students, for a series of inventory control management positions that were coming up. Many of those who attained positions at that time have since risen within the ranks of the company.

The Hotel and Restaurant program was a showpiece for the School. It received a great deal of publicity owing to its uniqueness as a

Legal Assistant class with faculty member Jack Flynn

Igor Sokur with students in the Hotel and Restaurant program

cooking program that was first and foremost about training managers for the industry. The concept opened many eyes, including those of the Royal Canadian Golf Association (RCGA). As a result, we had our first foray into the golf business.

"They saw that we were training these students for management positions," says Bev Walden. "They wanted their golf pros to be more than golfers – they wanted them to be managers. The RCGA believed they needed a broader range. A golf course at that time was something that closed for the winter so they knew they had to get into the catering and country club side to survive."

Retired Humber College Executive Vice President Tex Noble worked with the RCGA to start Golf Management as part of the Business Administration program. The program was given a push by Dean Mundinger, whose daughter was playing in the women's professional golf circuit in the States. But the RCGA began having difficulties with membership and the program was phased out in the late seventies.

There was still a need for a program of its kind, and we were ready when opportunity knocked again. In the late nineties, the School introduced a new Professional Golf Management program – one very similar in scope to the original. This time the industry partner was the Canadian Professional Golf Association.

In those early years, the Business School was particularly driven by its desire to connect with business. Because the future of every program depended on how well the market received graduates, the watchword of the day was "jobs". Faculty focused on connecting with industry to keep programs fresh and vital.

For that reason, the Business School was keen to develop agreements with professional associations. As a result of such an agreement, it became possible to complete the Accounting program at Humber and become a Certified General Accountant in a shorter period of time.

"In the seventies and eighties we solidified the relationship with the Canadian Chartered Accountants and the Society of Management Accountants," says John Liphardt. "They became linked effectively with Humber College, which gave Accounting grads strong recognition."

"The majority of our Accounting faculty were accredited – our standards were high," he says. "Faculty member Harvey Freedman worked at getting accounting and computer applications closely linked. He adjusted the program so it was an early adapter for computerization. It took a lot of hard work and

it couldn't have been done without him."

We also worked very closely with the Purchasing Management Association, and the Personnel Association of Ontario (now the Human Resources Professionals Association of Ontario).

Another important initiative was the creation of the Centre for Employee Benefits – more proof that the Business School was not only innovative, but also well connected to industry. James Brodie, who joined the faculty in 1967, developed the Centre. He came to Humber with contacts in the benefits industry, which was looking for a certificate program to keep employees up to date with current trends and legislation. John Wallace took over from Brodie and under his tutelage, the Centre rose to new heights.

But what was truly unique about the Centre in the late seventies was that it actually made money for the Business School – a first for the College.

David McPherson became Associate Director in 1980 and continues to teach for the Centre. He tells us, "Initially it was set up in 1969 to be a cost recovery department but it went on to become a revenue generating model. The Centre was bringing money in from private sources. Business became the first division that didn't depend on government grants alone."

The Centre was crucial to the benefits industry because change occurs so quickly. Aside from updating and refreshing benefits experts, though, the Centre also allows employers to promote staff into the benefits area by sending them for updating of relevant tax legislation and trends.

"It's a partnership with industry. When the Centre initially started, industry provided instructors while we managed administration and marked papers. It was a great innovation at the time because all the competing programs around were

Dean Mundinger (second from the left) makes a presentation in Igor's Dining Room

John Wallace (left) of the Centre for Employee Benefits

David McPherson (right) of the Centre for Employee Benefits

just seminars. Our Centre offered certification and correspondence programs, which meant people could take them from all over the country."

"The Centre brought recognition to us because everyone in the benefits industry knew we were offering this programming. It gave Humber a high profile in the business community."

Although the Centre was moved to the Business Development Division in 1994, it continues to grow and enjoy a great reputation across the country. In fact, it's thought to be the oldest employee benefits training program in Canada.

"Employers are very happy with the program," says McPherson. "They keep sending us people, and that's key because they're paying for employees to learn."

Another important way the Business School connected with employers was through the development of a Speaker's Forum, headed up

by John Liphardt.

"We'd get really good people from places like General Motors and Proctor and Gamble and we'd cancel classes and bring all the students together in the amphitheatre," says Liphardt. "It was very successful and one of the better ways we introduced students to the business community."

Also in the early seventies, Liphardt sold two major drug companies on the idea of seminars for their sales staff. He developed the course material and, with resources so scarce, he had to organize catering and register participants himself.

"It was so successful that the next year they brought in the entire sales force. For many faculty members it was a chance to work with active and highly successful salespeople and that gave us a lot of confidence in our classroom delivery."

"Eventually," adds Liphardt, "the College created an entire department to develop conferences and

seminars, but in the early days it was one more way for the Business School to work with industry."

History shows that the Business School was on the cutting edge of many ideas and trends. And in many instances we were simply too early. The prime example is our co-op programs.

"In the early seventies we offered at least three co-op programs," says Liphardt about a concept in programming that didn't truly blossom until the nineties. "We had co-op programs in retail management, wholesaling management and supermarket management. Students were on campus for a semester, then they'd work a semester, the same way co-op programs operate today."

"But these early co-op programs had to be phased out due to logistics. We simply didn't have the administration to supervise the programs."

Another concept the School was interested in very early was lifelong learning. In fact, from 1973 to 1975, Dean Mundinger was instrumental in developing interaction agreements with other post-secondary institutions, which opened doors for students to continue their education. He specifically worked on agreements with York and Ryerson that allowed many students to gain credits for advanced standing.

An agreement with Lakehead University in Thunder Bay was particularly groundbreaking. It allowed graduates with a 75 percent average to get a degree in business administration with just one additional year of study. Many who took advantage of this opportunity went on to complete postgraduate work — and at least one grad became a medical doctor.

Technology rears its head

Since technological advancement was a prime reason for the creation of community colleges, it's not surprising that computers played a key role in the development of the Business School – both academically and on the administrative side.

"When we started the College everything was paper based," says Bev Walden. "At the time, though, we only had a couple of hundred students. Over the first years or so some computer applications were written to support record keeping because we found out very quickly that we had to keep track of students' records in perpetuity."

"The immense volume of information to come meant we had to organize a series of programs. The evolution has been going on for 30 years and still hasn't finished. We went from a system of handwriting names on a list, to a keypunch system, to an automated system called CHRIS – where people can register for courses using a touchtone phone."

"In the seventies, computers allowed us to see what percentage of students were taking which courses. That improved our ability to provide better customer service for students. We could see what they wanted so we were better prepared to provide it."

Academically, the Business School was on the sharp edge of change. This was the first school in the province to offer computer programming. Initiated in 1968, it was sponsored by the federal government to meet the burgeoning need for computers in the workplace. Eventually the program was opened up to fee-paying students before moving to the Technology Division in the late seventies.

Dave Haisell was hired away from IBM, along with Bev Walden, in 1968 to develop the computer programming area. It grew quickly, keeping pace with the expansion of computer technology and always fighting for more resources!

"When I started there were two classes in computer programming," says Haisell, who became Chair of Information Systems in 1978. "The program eventually expanded and gave birth to other program variations, including co-op and certificate programs."

"Faculty had to use their own initiative to remain current. The industry changed every semester and if faculty didn't keep pace the students caught on. We were lucky in that we had a very involved advisory committee that influenced our thinking and provided invaluable support. They were also employers and if grads weren't up to snuff they let us know."

But with all the opportunities of the sparkling new computer era came new fears. In the beginning, there was reluctance in some programs to give up courses in order to accommodate computer courses. There was fear among faculty about being able to remain current because the field was changing so rapidly. And there was fear

A Humber computer lab in the 1970s

"Eventually we got some capital and bought a mini-computer," says Walden. "We used it for demos. Then we bought 20 Commodore computers, and linked them together to create a small network. Students used them to run mortgage programs to calculate compound interest – and, of course, some used them to play Pacman."

"This was the first real computer lab, although we also had labs where students could keypunch data and take it to a mainframe. Eventually it opened up to other divisions and soon after it blossomed," says Walden.

Don Wheeler remembers using one of the early computers to impress prospective students and parents. "When the College had an Open House in the early seventies, a computer mysteriously appeared in the room where the Business School was presenting. We hooked it up to the telephones and were able to use it to highlight what we were

teaching. For many people, it was the first computer they had seen so it was a real glimpse of the future and it created some genuine excitement about education."

And it's that spirit of anticipation that truly encapsulates the decade.

The seventies offered the Business School all the characteristics of youth: experimentation, enthusiasm and unbridled growth. It was a time when there were no limitations on what we could accomplish. And driven as we were by a belief in our purpose, we soared.

in administration of not being able to supply enough funds.

The outlay of money was daunting. Bev Walden says the expense of equipping the College with computers was overwhelming, especially in the early seventies. The computer facilities available to students grew slowly at first,

along with the budget.

"The first computers that students could work on by themselves were three teletypes hooked up to a system at George Brown College – the only college at that time that had a dial-up facility."

Building Business A History of the Business School at Humber

Chapter 3 | The 80s: Strategy

Live out your imagination, not your history.

STEPHEN COVEY

Presidents Gordon Wragg (left) and Dr. Robert A. (Squee) Gordon

With the new decade came a change in attitude. The unrestrained growth of the seventies was at long last harnessed as the Business School entered an era of strategy. Growth for the sake of growth was no longer acceptable – it had to be managed and planned for.

Perhaps much of the change in management started at the top. In 1981, Gordon Wragg — the long-standing and much-loved President of the College – retired. New at the helm was Dr. Robert A. Gordon, a President whose academic background and CGEP experience brought a new quality to all facets of Humber, including the Business School.

Accountability became paramount. The Business School was more answerable both to senior administration and, ultimately, to legislature as the recession of 1981 brought more students than ever to our doors. By that time, the College had grown so big that we were running out of space.

"It was a time of significant expansion," says David Murray. One of the first graduating students from the Business School, Murray was a member of the Board of Governors from 1982 to 1989, and eventually became Chair. "The Board met every two weeks and we always had a full slate. A lot of building went on and allocating funds for program expansion was always an issue. We discussed the value of programs and their contribution to society in order to make decisions."

"Humber was growing so much it was clear we had to do something. It was apparent the city was growing north, so we considered buying a farm north of us. We also considered stacked parking lots. In the end, we decided to build a residence. And that was when we first entered into discussions to attain the Lakeshore Psychiatric Facility in order to expand that campus."

The strategic growth continued until the end of the decade, when an economic crunch affected College funding.

Says Murray, "Squee [President Gordon] was brilliant in terms of where the ship should go without the usual financing. Suddenly, stretching the dollar was a concern. Growth shifted more than it slowed. Some facilities could not be expanded and we had to get more inventive about how we wanted to spend our money."

David Murray, Board Chair

But until then, the Business School continued to flourish, taking the College into some exciting – and uncharted – new territory.

The growth of International Programs

John Liphardt, Dean from 1981 to 1987, took every opportunity to move the School in new directions. As a result, the eighties saw the development of many new programs, new markets for students and new ways to deliver education. One of the most significant ways he extended the reach of the Business School was to take it overseas.

In the fall of 1982, Liphardt approached Tom Norton, Vice President Academic, and let him know the Business School was interested in international projects. Norton, who had been in discussions with the Association of Canadian Community Colleges (ACCC) and the Canadian International Development Agency (CIDA), revealed that the Chinese government wanted to establish five separate management training centres in China, each one developed by a different G7 country. Norton and Liphardt were eager to see Humber involved.

"The idea was to train middle- to senior-level managers in North American business methods and studies," says Liphardt. "We had only two weeks to get 12 faculty to develop 12 courses."

In March of 1983, Liphardt went to China to sell the program developed by the Business School. He was successful and, as a result, several Humber faculty members headed to China to teach.

According to Toby Fletcher, the Business School's involvement makes perfect sense from an historical perspective. He says that Canada and Canada's post-secondary education system were viewed very favourably around the world at that time.

"Canadian businesses were asserting themselves internationally and we were learning that Canada had to step forward and become a player," says Fletcher, who joined the Business School in the early eighties and eventually became Associate Dean. "We were getting international jurisdictions interested in Canadian training because they were looking at us and saying, 'How did little tiny Canada get to be part of the G7?'"

"At the time we had the highest participation rate in post-secondary education in the world, meaning that more Canadian high school students were going on to college or university. Other countries were looking at us and asking what we were doing right."

"So there was a wave of globalization and the Business School was riding it. And it helped that we were well connected."

John Murray, Marketing Professor from 1982 to 1992, helped develop and teach the curriculum for the management training centre, which was built about 3,000 miles inland, in the city of Cheng-du in Szechuan province. He worked as part of a team of six, which included fellow faculty member Phil Wright, two teachers from a college in Alberta and two from a college in the Maritimes.

"Before 1982, China was closed to the world, so it was all so new to us," he says.

"No one spoke English, we had to work with sequential interpreters. At the time, China was made up of huge state enterprises and complete families were part of these business organizations for life. We taught 85 students from different enterprises, ranging in age from 30 to 75. It was their first taste of North American business."

The program was comprised of many of the same elements as the regular Business Administration program, including human resources, accounting, and product development. While based on our existing material, the curriculum was tailored to the very unique needs of Chinese enterprises.

"In terms of learning," says Murray, "they thought some of our ideas were from the moon, but we made a dent. The Cheng-du Centre of Management Training was the first business school set up by North Americans in China, and we're proud of that."

Aside from the professional accomplishments, there was much to be gained personally.

"It was a wonderful experience," he says. "They gave us a trip down the Yangtze River, which you can't do today because of dams. We roared around the streets exploring the country on bikes. Everyone was dressed in dark navy blue Mao suits – except the kids, who were brightly dressed. That's changing now."

The success of those early efforts can be measured by the enthusiasm of the Chinese government to work with Humber on future projects. In fact, the Business School now teaches Business Administration at Ningbo University in eastern China – and students come to Humber for their third year of studies.

With a successful experience in China under our belt, the Business School was eager to expand international offerings. Another opportunity was

International students on a cultural outing in Ottawa

quick to present itself when, in the mid-eighties, Yaro Sokolyk, a prominent member of the Ukrainian Community in Toronto, approached President Gordon and urged Humber College to establish a partnership with a polytechnic in the Ukraine — the Kyiv State University of Trade and Economics.

After a visit to Canada by the President of the Ukraine, senior officials and faculty of the university, an agreement was reached for short-term faculty exchanges. A formal signing ceremony was held at Humber.

Our first step was to gather over a thousand textbooks emphasizing entrepreneurship to enhance their library. Then Business School faculty members Ihor Sokolyk and Anne Harper visited Kiev to learn as much as possible from economics, management and accounting faculty. That meant they could enrich studies at home by bringing examples into their classes of the Ukraine's struggles to move to a market economy – a unique benefit for our students.

"This project took place at a very turbulent time in the Ukraine's history," explains Toby Fletcher. "It began just before the fall of the Berlin Wall in November 1989, and the collapse of the Soviet Union. As a result, the Ukraine declared independence and, with the help of CIDA funding, the project expanded in the early nineties to include the Centre for Productivity in Kramatorsk and Industry Canada."

The Director, senior officials, and faculty visited Humber College several times over three years. Eventually they established a Centre for Entrepreneurship and Small Business in the Ukraine.

Faculty at the Centre began the annual publication of a professional journal. CIDA funded the purchase and installation of three desktop computers and software, and the Business School provided textbooks and resource materials, as well as a business plan for the new Centre.

Sadly, though, the Business School's work with the Ukraine fizzled out later in the nineties.

"The Ukraine sank into chaos and it became difficult to manage the program. It was a shame," laments Fletcher. "It had tremendous human intellectual capital in space technology and other high tech areas."

In the late eighties, funding from CIDA through ACCC enabled the Business School to establish an exchange program with St. Vincent Technical College on the island of St. Vincent. Through the program, we shared our expertise in office administration, computer skills, small business and enterprise development, library administration, college administration, college-level academic program development and college teaching techniques.

Says Fletcher, "Faculty and administrators from the Business School traveled to St. Vincent at least once a year to lecture and consult on Canadian business and college teaching practices. What's more, for three straight

Alvina Cassiani, Dean Hatton (centre) and a delegation from Shanghai

years, the Business School went there to host a faculty professional development event called 'the Great Teachers' Conference' at the beginning of their fall term, which was a terrific success."

Jack Buckley, Dean from 1987 to 1990, says about the St. Vincent program: "Many, many students came to Humber, then went back to their island and made significant contributions. We had a big presence there for many years. We set up a computer lab that was the first one in any educational institution on the island."

The beginning of postgraduate programs

The first postgraduate program to emerge from the Business School was a natural. The relationships with industry and professional associations that had begun in the seventies were still going strong, and none was stronger than the relationship with

the Personnel Association (now the Human Resources Professionals Association of Ontario).

"One of the strengths of the Business School is that it was always going after associations to validate education," says Toby Fletcher. "Partnering is a strength. And the idea works so well because all professional associations – from doctors and lawyers to welders – have the same model. They're all based on education, experience and validation."

"[Chair] Don Wheeler and I were active in professional associations," says Fletcher. "At the time, all of the new ideas from the Personnel Association of Ontario were coming out of the Toronto Chapter, which we were affiliated with. The philosophy of this chapter was that all types of human resources, including compensation, pension and so on, should join forces."

And they did. The personnel sector began to

change dramatically in the mid-eighties as it became more about people and management, less about tracking data.

The creation of a formidable new industry spelled opportunity for the Business School. That we were going to have an expanded role was a given, considering we were already leading the way in human resources training.

"The Personnel Association of Toronto knew us in the Business School and so together we looked for ways to manage change in the industry," says Fletcher.

"At the same time, it was interesting to us that university graduates with arts degrees were the ones getting into human resources. And it was also interesting that they were exactly who employers were looking for. So the development of a postgraduate program geared to these students, while a new concept, was simply a matter of meeting a need in the

Dr. John Murray, faculty member

marketplace."

The development of the fast-track postgraduate Human Resource Management program geared to university graduates began in 1985. Doreen Bell, Coordinator of the Human Resource Management courses and profile, was instrumental in researching and collecting the data necessary for the approval of this unique program. Once the program was approved, Doreen visited job fairs at various universities to inform graduating students of the new program. A key selling feature was the advanced standing students would receive towards their professional designation in the human resources field.

While it started with just 25 applicants, in a few years that number had skyrocketed to 500. It became one of the fastest growing programs in the college system.

Professor John Murray noticed that many students in his marketing class were university graduates. It turned out that marketing was another great fit for the postgraduate format.

"We talked to young people who had graduated from university in liberal arts who didn't even know how to get started looking for jobs. All these people had needs that weren't being met. Once the postgraduate Marketing Management program was developed, we went to universities to drum up business, but after two years we didn't need to. They were coming to us."

According to Murray, the postgraduate programs are successful because they offer a small class size and an environment that closely mirrors business. "For the Marketing Management program, we broke the class into small groups of four to six so they could work as they do in industry, analyzing issues and making presentations."

"We learned that these people were turned on by their studies. They came to us with little confidence and minimal business skills and became very motivated."

Postgraduate programs continue to be a key component of the Business School. As we head into the 21st century, the development of more postgraduate programs is a renewed priority.

Advisory committees and leadership

Murray credits the Business School with an "openness" that allowed faculty to experiment with new ideas for teaching business.

Advisory Committee members Fred Nogas, Senior Consultant, Feldman Gray and Associates, and Mitch Champagne (top), Senior Manager, Deloitte & Touche LLP

"The faculty were encouraged to experiment, and that's how I became interested in the idea of leadership. At the time it wasn't taught as a course in colleges or universities. But I had a lot of contacts in the business world and I learned that the Marketing program was a little out of sync with business."

He tells us that the Conference Board of Canada was lamenting the lack of employability skills such as leadership, problem solving, oral and written communication and prioritizing, among the youth entering the business community. It was clear to Murray that these skills had to be incorporated into his curriculum to better meet the needs of industry.

"I designed a course in business leadership that was pretty popular with students," he says. "I didn't do so much lecturing as much as I dumped problems on small groups of students. They had to present their findings to the class, which was more in tune with what was happening in industry."

Murray used his contacts at Shell, Imperial Oil, Bank of Montreal, General Electric and Ernst & Young to form a powerhouse of an advisory committee. While all programs have advisory committees made up of professionals who guide the curriculum, the marketing group met more frequently than most and took on more responsibilities.

"When we listened to these people, what they had to say was different from the textbook. We worked together very intensively, meeting every three or four weeks for about a year and a half. They were heavily involved with the curriculum. They put together a presentation on the new skills that businesses would require for the nineties and it didn't relate to what we were teaching. John Riccio, who was Chair at the time, decided that the curricula for all the courses had to be rewritten. In terms of content, it was a new direction for the Business School."

John Riccio agrees that Murray and his illustrious advisory committee had a huge impact on the Business School.

"We focused on employability skills across the board in the eighties. The transition took about seven years to complete," says Riccio. "I felt that in order to differentiate our students and make them better employees and future leaders, they needed these skills. I believed these skills should be delivered in such a way that they build throughout the program. The process was a partnership among administration, faculty and an excellent group of advisory committee members – they were very active and made many presentations to our faculty members. They were the driving force."

Adds Riccio, "Now more and more colleges are focusing on employability skills."

Liphardt agrees that the Marketing Advisory Committee was very influential. He tells us that, while he was Dean, he insisted that advisory committees work hard to keep the programs in touch with the realities of the industries they're designed to serve.

"The members knew the programs well. We made sure advisory committees were very active because they brought credibility to the programs and in their networking they helped spread the word. The advisory committees had to be critical and they had to be strong."

The student-centred approach

Programs that had remained the same since their inception began to change during Liphardt's tenure as Dean. Strategic adjustments made in the mid-eighties were the beginning of a trend that would continue until the end of the decade.

"I made sure that most programs had a three-year venue," says Liphardt, who added an optional third year to the Accounting, Marketing, Data Processing and Computer programs. "It was partly competitive. And

we felt students would have more credits for university, meaning they'd spend less time at university and more at Humber. Students responded well to it."

The Business School was always very good at giving students what they want, but by the end of the eighties a College-wide edict made it official. The College was shifting policies away from faculty-centred priorities toward student-centred ones.

It was a commitment to the best policies for student success, including orientation, registration, student advising, transfer among programs during and following the first year, and student awards.

But the Business School had its own ideas about being student-centred. For instance, a move to early registration whereby students chose their own timetables was a major innovation. And, in an unprecedented move, an academic counsellor was

stationed within the School's offices.

Counsellor Martin Pieke was given the task of changing the way students in the Business School thought about getting help.

"Students weren't aware of counseling and so they weren't using it," says Pieke. "We thought that if a counsellor was in the Business School offices, students would make more effective use of the service." Having a counsellor

on hand was a platform to achieve many changes.

"At the same time all divisions wanted more of a counsellor presence, but the Business School was the only one that provided an office. Counseling became a person and not just a department. We were trying to reach students at risk – students who didn't have a sense of how to get help. And we were trying to move the student services area to the forefront."

"The faculty were also positive about a counsellor being present right in the Business School offices. If a student had a concern, there was easy access to advice. My door was always open," says Pieke, who was often invited to department faculty and management meetings to discuss student issues.

During the same period, a number of projects and programs were initiated to meet student needs. One pilot project saw Pieke and Toby Fletcher interview each first semester student twice during the 1988 winter semester to not only identify problems, but also to initiate early intervention. The pair presented the program and its results at the College's 1989 Innovations Showcase and at the National Institute for Staff and Organizational Development (NISOD).

"We felt good about the project," says Pieke. "It gave us the incentive to do more. We learned that if every student in first semester had a

faculty advisor it would make the transition to college less daunting."

Fletcher adds, "We put more thought into students' needs at the beginning of the educational process. We determined where their skills were weak and that helped us ensure their success."

Pieke also asked faculty to identify early in the semester any student who appeared to be at risk, and he contacted students with failing marks at mid-term and offered to meet with them and discuss possible ways to raise their marks.

Other initiatives included in-class study skills workshops, an orientation for business students during which the professional options of each program were carefully outlined, a brief presentation in every freshman class on student services and counselling services, and a presentation at an orientation session for parents.

"We learned that personal contact was more important than all the leaflets and flyers and posters. But it was impossible to maintain with such limited resources," says Pieke.

In another important move, the Business School established a common first year for its Accounting, Business Management, Business Administration, Computer Information Systems, and Marketing diploma programs in 1989. By doing so, students had more flexibility and were less likely to drop out.

"Many students didn't know what they wanted," says Fletcher. "The common first year gave them a foundation. In the past, students would take a program and drop out if it didn't suit them, but now they had the option of transferring to another program without a disadvantage."

In a strategic move that year, the Business School established a January intake

to try to capture "semestered" high school students. The idea also worked well as a retention strategy because it allowed students who would drop out at the end of their first semester to begin a new program in January without missing a beat.

The January intake started small but today the Business School takes in more first-semester students in January than some schools do in September.

The idea was so popular, in fact, that later that year the Business School initiated Summer College – essentially, opening the doors for a third intake session. While the idea of opening the College in the summer was not new to the Business School, we finally had the resources to operate full tilt during the summer months and offer students a full range of services.

The student-centred philosophy also found its way into the curriculum of individual programs. The

Business Administration program gave its students more control over their lives with what was affectionately called the "cafeteria approach" to curriculum.

Toby Fletcher tells us, "The cafeteria idea was simple: every student needed a balanced meal – an appetizer, a drink, an entree with vegetables, and dessert. The student could select from choices in each category to assemble an array of courses that met the curriculum requirements and suited the student's wants and needs."

"We felt strongly that this approach helped students participate in their education and, with some guidance and advice, made them feel that the program met their idea of what they wanted in a business education. At the same time, we were able to ensure that each student received a foundation in the basic functions and disciplines of business."

In and out of fashion

In 1980, there was a major programming switch. The Hotel and Restaurant program was transferred to the (now non-existent) Applied Arts Division and the Retail Co-op program was transferred out of Applied Arts and into the Business School.

Retail Co-op had its roots in a program from the early seventies that combined family studies, food, and fashion. In the mid-seventies it was split into two programs: Fashion Careers and Family Studies. Then Fashion Careers split into a business program (Retail Co-op) and a modeling program (Fashion) that remained in Applied Arts.

With the modeling component removed from Retail Co-op, it had a different tone and attracted more business-minded students. The move to the Business School in 1980 reflected

its new direction. Shortly afterwards, the name of the program was changed to Retail Management, to coincide with Ministry guidelines, although the program remained a co-op, offering students paid work terms in retail stores and shops.

"The Retail Management program suffered from economic cycles," says Laurie Turner, who started teaching in the program in the mid-seventies and remained on faculty in that program until she became Coordinator of Business Administration in 1993. "Grads had difficulty getting jobs when the economy was tough but it was hard getting students in boom times. And in the good times, employers just scooped them up from the program during co-ops."

Meanwhile, the Fashion program in Applied Arts continued to evolve. The modeling aspect was dropped and the focus was now on cosmetics and event production. In fact,

The Fashion program staged many successful events, like this one in 2002

2001 Fashion event
"Synthesis" at the
Guvernment

warrant two years of college education. So, in 1996, the Retail Management program was cancelled, leaving the field wide open for the Fashion program, which began positioning itself as "the business of fashion."

History soon repeated itself. The Fashion program was transferred to the Business School where it continues to blossom.

Credentialism is fuelled

When it came to hiring staff in the seventies, there was an emphasis on retaining professionals who were well connected with industry. The Business School was so focused on jobs for students that it placed tremendous value on contacts and experience – facets that spoke highly to employers about the quality of the practical education students were receiving.

Simply put, academic credentials paled beside a high-ranking title from a prestigious organization.

Should a prospective faculty member have a graduate-level education, it was an asset – but one that was seen as being limited in its usefulness.

The strategy to hire better-credentialed faculty and administrators began in the early eighties with Dr. Gordon as President. At that time there were a number of people who didn't have graduate level credentials. Indeed, many Business School faculty members continued to insist that practical experience was far more relevant to students.

The issue garnered more attention in the early to mid-nineties with downsizing and layoffs. There were few opportunities to hire new people and it became very clear that credentialed applicants were winning the majority of positions. Since 1997, there has been a very clear strategic policy that favours credentialed applicants.

Chair from 1988 to 2002, Toby Fletcher did a great deal of hiring – and he put a big

it morphed into something like the original Retail Management program and the two programs became quite competitive for students.

As the economy improved, the Fashion program flourished as students were drawn to

glamorous careers. Yet, the Retail Management program began to suffer as it struggled for enrollment.

Administration began to think that the starting salaries in the retail sector were so low that they didn't

emphasis on the letters that appeared after an individual's name.

"I felt strongly that credentials were the product of the Business School," says Fletcher. "And if our business was credentials, we had to value them."

"If I were asked what we were selling, I'd say it's confidence – confidence that we provide the best education and training in the field as well as confidence on the part of employers. When they get a resume that says Humber on it, we want them to know that piece of paper is worth something."

"If I were asked to present an image of the Business School, I'd say it's bold and confident. Bold because we are willing to take risks, but it also implies competence and perseverance, which are reflected in credentials."

Into the nineties, the issue took on growing importance with our students. Indeed, owing to partnerships with

organizations like the HRPAO that made it easier for students to become accredited upon graduation, we were able to promote credentialism among prospective students. And it proved to be a strong draw.

"The credential we offer is more powerful if it's accredited by an association," says Fletcher. "We built curriculum for that credential."

Our office is transformed by technology

In the early eighties, the Business School office staff used electric typewriters. The focus of the office was the infamous "typing basket" where ten full-time administrative staff and 100

full-time faculty members left their tests, class notes, and everything else that needed to be typed. When a secretary or assistant finished whatever task she was working on, she always had the typing basket to turn to for a never-ending supply of work.

Even worse, though, was the hand-cranked ditto copying machine that emitted such terrible fumes that the staff worried about its affect on their health. They eventually purchased a Xerox machine but it was so expensive to operate that staff were limited in the number of copies they were allowed to make.

In 1989, the first personal computers arrived in the office.

"It was like heaven," says Sharon Schembri, who started with the Business School in 1981. "It meant you were more confident about your work and you were using your time more wisely. It was much easier. And you were more independent because you

spent less time in teams doing chores like collating."

Another issue that plagued the staff – and students – were line-ups that ran out the office doors and down the hall for five to six weeks at the beginning of every school year. It was the only way students could add or drop courses.

At that time each division registered their own students, who were given six cards to hand in, one for each of their courses. Data control would then key punch each card to get the number of students in each course. Elective sheets were posted in the concourse with information such as room, time and instructor, and it was up to the student to check for the details they needed.

In the mid-eighties a computerized system called SHAR was introduced to the College and the Registrar's Office took over the registration process. From that point on, the Business School was only responsible for handing out timetables.

Line-ups diminished.

"It was much better," says Schembri. "Students weren't coming in as much with problems, they went down to the Registrar's Office where they could add and drop courses quickly. There was less frustration for everyone."

The computer era is good for some programs, bad for others.

From the seventies to the mid-eighties, our Office Administration (secretarial) programs were among our most successful academic endeavours. They burgeoned and grew along with industry demand. But the advent of personal computers changed all that, and for droves of women who would otherwise have found themselves in the "pink ghetto" of low-paying administrative jobs, doors of opportunity flew open.

"There was once a huge demand for secretarial people but that changed a lot. For almost 20 years we had large, viable programs taught in the day and evening," says John Liphardt.

Elsie Swartz addresses Legal Secretary program graduates at Convocation

It wasn't the demand alone that made our programs grow. In many cases the faculty of the Office Administration programs had gained the attention of industry.

"Most noteworthy was the Legal Secretary program," says Liphardt. "One faculty member, Elsie Swartz, was a legal secretary of renown. She wrote the definitive textbook for legal secretaries in Canada. We thought so much of her we asked her to do the convocation address."

In the business community, our secretarial programs enjoyed a great reputation, partially because they managed to stay on the leading edge of innovation.

"The secretarial programs were very progressive in bringing in word processing and working with IBM. At one point IBM agreed to use us as a test case for word processing." Liphardt laughs, "I remember it took about 20 IBM technicians a week to get the equipment up and running. But at the time it was very progressive."

"And it was the secretarial group that started the Telecommunications program," he adds. "Chair

Joan Girvan knew it would be important. Joan also developed distance learning so people across the country could take telecommunications courses."

Pat Hudson joined the College in 1976 and remains on faculty with the Business School. She tells us that from 1978 to 1980, there was a significant curriculum change in our Office Administration programs.

"We moved away from general courses," says Hudson. "In the beginning we had two semesters of general and one semester of specialization. But we switched it so students had one semester of general and two of specialization."

"This was one of the first colleges to be more specialized. Employers responded very positively. At times we had five posted jobs for every student. Because neurologists and psychiatrists, and other specialists have very specific terminology, and since our medical-secretarial students were getting a better grasp of the differences, employers appreciated the fact that we had more of a focus."

"Also, it was more interesting to students," says Hudson. "I remember at that time they were teaching secretarial courses in high school, so students came to us with some general skills – what they wanted and needed was specialization."

"The colleges were very competitive for the best students so we could market ourselves as distinctive. But eventually, other colleges followed suit."

The Business School was determined to stay on top of the heap. As a result, a lot of money was invested in the Office Administration programs.

"We also had a word processing program. There was a big market for it because in those days a business might have a whole floor of word processor operators where the department sent work for word processing. In our lab we had Micom systems – each cost about $100,000. Employers like Bell Canada were coming to us because we had this system. In those days different systems weren't compatible, so it was very important to find graduates who had training on the same systems you had. And back then we were the only ones who had Micom."

"In the late seventies and early eighties when we were teaching word processing there was enormous demand. But it wasn't until 1986 that we pushed the administration to include a room of personal computers. To get 25 to 30 stations was a huge investment. We had to convince the College that it was what the business community wanted. Even in an educational institution, that was a difficult thing."

"Many people were still hesitant about computers," says Hudson. "I remember when I worked at the Keelesdale campus in the late seventies and we had one computer. I had to introduce it to students and faculty and everyone was afraid of it. At that time, no one realized how it would transform our lives."

The early eighties were glory days of growth for Office Administration. But by the end of the decade, the bloom was off the rose as the need for graduates faded. The advent of the personal computer (PC) meant that managers no longer needed their own assistants – they were expected to initiate their own documents.

"The PC changed our reality," says Hudson. "The evolution of personal computers became part of the downsizing of companies where we see computers take the place of positions. So in the early nineties, the decision was made to do away with the secretarial programs."

The Legal Secretary program was the last to go in 1998, although there's still a Law Firm Profile, a joint venture with major Toronto law firms. Graduates from that program are still in demand today because lawyers are unique in their need for skills like transcribing.

"So secretaries disappeared," she says. "Titles changed to things like administrative assistant, executive assistant, administrative manager. In that realm most people work for a group of managers rather than an individual."

The end of the demand for secretaries changed the student body of the Business School. Suddenly women were coming here in droves to learn how to be managers and entrepreneurs – rather than to be the support for others with those ambitions.

"Today no one wants to be a data entry operator," says Hudson. "Students say it's boring and has no future, so young women are coming into the business programs instead."

"Women make up a greater percentage of the workplace now. In the seventies women took jobs for a short period and didn't intend to stay. Many companies asked you to leave when you got married so, of course, they didn't offer women benefits or pensions."

"The concept of lifelong learning has affected women. Today you have to be self-sufficient and what's more, to stay in the field of technology – which has replaced so many of the secretarial positions – you have to keep learning new programs and new technology."

Not only has Hudson seen a change in the attitudes of female students, she has seen a change in the attitudes among her peers.

"Early on, women didn't apply for management positions. I remember being told by a friend that I shouldn't bother to apply for the position of coordinator because they would probably hire a man. But I was encouraged by two men in the Business School to apply and I got the position."

"In the eighties women moved to more managerial positions as management fostered a positive attitude and it became more progressive. But it's a societal thing," says Hudson. "As society starts to change, so do its institutions."

Equity comes to the Business School

The continuous marketing of Business School graduates was paying dividends in so many different ways. By the start of the eighties there were ten graduating classes from the three-year Business Administration group. Earlier graduates were now in positions of authority and were returning to recruit graduating students. Many had become actively involved in their professional associations.

When the Ontario government introduced Pay Equity, our connections with graduates proved valuable.

The College was approached to provide assistance and guidance to the commission in developing the teaching package that would be necessary to bring various companies on board with the legislation. Doreen Bell and Anne Harper, members of the Management Studies faculty, were seconded to the Ministry and the Business School became a key player in developing the Pay Equity workshops that were to be conducted throughout the province. Among the first group to be certified to conduct the Pay Equity workshops were Anne Harper, Doreen Bell, David McPherson, Toby Fletcher and Don Wheeler.

Our involvement in the real world meant that the Business School would continue to be at the forefront of business and industry. At the same time, students recognized that they were receiving current information and skills. In fact, many

Businesss School faculty member Shirley Harrison works with a student in the computer lab

and assistance as programs were developed in a variety of business sectors from health care management to supermarket management.

Many faculty members aided in the design and development of courses as well as in delivering courses on behalf of Corporate Education Services. Our involvement began in the early days with the Training in Business and Industry (TIBI) Division, the forerunner to corporate services. Over the years, the Business School has been an active supporter of many of these company-specific training programs.

It was in the eighties, however, that our involvement flourished. That was when computers became an essential tool in modern human resource management. The Business School developed a unique liaison with Comshare, a leading company of the day, in the development of human resource computer software.

Business School graduates were now members of the School's various advisory committees working to keep curricula relevant.

Partnering with industry

The Business School saw itself as a team player and was often instrumental in bringing potential clients to other areas of the College. One of the key areas was Corporate Education Services. Faculty members were able to provide key contact names

This cooperative effort, the first of its kind between the industry leader and a community college, was of great benefit to students enrolled in the Business Administration, Business Management and Information Systems programs.

The College's 140 microcomputer units were equipped with the Comshare Human Resource Information System, Profiles/PC, via a local area network. The package was designed to simplify the handling of personnel functions like applicant tracking, record keeping, labour relations, payroll, benefits administration, and access to key decision-making reports.

"Human resources staff have been almost the last company employees to become involved with computers," said Dan Manherz, Comshare's Director of Marketing Support, at the time. "We believe that by offering Profiles/PC as a training tool at Humber College, we can help reduce some of the human resource managers' fear of computers and, at the same time, teach them how to improve the productivity of their own departments as well as that of the whole company."

Profiles/PC was a complete human resource management system for companies of almost any size. Tied to the network of the day, many students could be trained at one time. Also, because the package was versatile, it could be tailored to the needs of individual companies. As a result, students who trained on the system acquired greater microcomputer flexibility, giving them a real edge when they entered the business world.

The Business School was also actively involved with the Comshare Profiles/PC Users Group that consisted of well over thirty companies. In fact, we often acted as host for the group's meetings. This proactive approach kept us at the forefront of recognition.

By the eighties, partnerships were developing in a variety of ways. One unique partnership that came about due to the successes of graduates of the seventies was the involvement of Business Administration students (and later the Human Resource Management students) with the Weston and District (now Metro West) Human Resources Association.

As a result of the growth of its membership and new concepts in compensation management, the Association recognized it had to streamline and modernize its annual salary and benefit survey which was conducted on behalf of the membership. Of particular importance was an overall analysis of the survey results.

Since members of the executive of the Association had been acting as advisory committee members in the Business School, it was natural to involve Business Administration students in the project. They assisted in the development of a written survey that would include salary and benefit questions, they collected data, and they tabulated and analyzed data.

Students studying in an applied college of arts and technology were given an opportunity to work on a live case and interact with business people as part of the development of their education. It was synergy at its best.

Partnerships may not have been new to the Business School, but they were really starting to pay off.

And no wonder. The eighties brought with it a focused mindset: a determination to control and manage the Business School. Coupled with a desire to explore new territory, this strategic approach to management led to major innovation as we became pioneers in areas of international programming, postgraduate education and technology.

But as the eighties drew to a close, austerity was in the air. Purse strings were closing and our urge to grow was harnessed by the need for restraint.

At the same time, many of the stalwart individuals who brought the Business School from its beginnings were approaching retirement age. Youth was about to bring a fresh perspective, and that would bring massive change.

The graduating class of the Human Resources postgraduate program from the spring of 1990

The Business School at the Lakeshore Campus

Today business programs at the North and Lakeshore campuses are run concurrently under the guidance of the Dean of the Business School. But for decades the two campuses seemed worlds apart – physically, philosophically and programmatically.

The North campus has always been the hub of activity and the primary location for post-secondary studies. Lakeshore, on the other hand, started out offering federally-funded college preparation and upgrading programs to older, more mature students who were sponsored by Unemployment Insurance.

In the mid-seventies, when the College acquired the building now known as Lakeshore, post-secondary diploma programs were then offered. The lineup included Business Administration, Business Management, Microcomputer Business Applications, Accounting, as well as Office Administration in English and French.

But, in the hearts and minds of Humber staff and faculty, Lakeshore remained a campus primarily designed to "retool" adults for the workforce.

"The issue in the late seventies was trying to develop an identity for ourselves," says John Ricco, who joined the Lakeshore faculty in 1976, and went on to become Chairman.

According to Riccio, the College considered expanding diploma business programs at Lakeshore but there was resistance. While the existing programs were basically a duplication of those offered at the North, some worried that the quality at Lakeshore wasn't at par. What's more, it was a struggle to convince administration that students coming from Mississauga and downtown Toronto comprised a big enough market for the campus.

"My role as chair was to carve out a niche for Lakeshore business programs. Eventually, the niche came naturally as we became the microcomputer specialists of the College," says Riccio.

In the late seventies – during the very early stages of the personal computer – Riccio had eight Commodore PETs. In a few years he had built an entire lab. His work with computers was so unique that he was profiled on CITY TV and CFRB radio.

In fact, faculty at the Lakeshore campus pioneered early computer courses, and were among the first to offer training in DOS 1, Lotus 1.0, WordPerfect 1 and several accounting packages.

"I told them at the North that they could keep the mainframe computer programs," laughs Riccio about his foray into the world of personal computers. "Microcomputers provided the focus around which the other business programs at Lakeshore were developed."

Indeed, the Microcomputer Business Applications program was so leading edge that new software was arriving one day and being taught the next. Although there weren't many computers around in those days, Riccio proved resourceful at finding them. He even had Xerox donate one of only ten existing STAR workstations – the basis for what became the Apple. Complete with mouse and icons, it was well before its time.

The biggest problem seemed to be letting the world know about the exciting technological advancements at Lakeshore. The public was still skeptical about microcomputers – even the funding specialist from the Ministry of Education didn't believe there would be jobs. But students always seemed to find the program and it thrived. The campus, however, remained primarily a location for retraining.

Until the late seventies, both campuses led very independent existences. They rarely communicated. But administration

Lakeshore

decided that programs offered by both campuses should have identical curricula, making communication between campuses a necessity. Keeping the programs similar, however, was an ongoing struggle.

Jack Buckley, Dean from 1987 to 1990, says, "Trying to keep curricula consistent between the two campuses so that the graduates of one were equally as competent as the graduates of the other was a big challenge. Accountability changed frequently."

Riccio agrees. "I reported to Richard Hook at Lakeshore. Then I reported to the North. At some points I reported to two deans. It was all over the place."

Change came fast and furious to the Lakeshore campus in the late eighties when government funding for retraining programs was dramatically reduced. Many faculty members were transferred to the North campus. It also became necessary to attract more students.

"We started to develop profiles unique to Lakeshore so the campus would become a destination for students from high school," says Pat Meek, who joined the faculty in 1981 and became coordinator of the Business Administration and Business Management programs at Lakeshore in 1988. Today Meek is Associate Dean of Business at the Lakeshore campus.

"We began with a co-op profile for the Business Administration program. It was extremely popular and attractive to well-qualified high school students. It was very strategic," says Meek. She worked closely with Michael Hatton, who was then responsible for the development of unique programs at Lakeshore.

The new program offered Business Administration students a paid co-op experience during both summer terms. With the exception of the co-op placements, the curriculum was identical to that at the North.

There were always more applications than available seats.

The current look for the renovated Cottages at the Lakeshore campus

Lakeshore campus library

While the number of co-op placements that could be secured limited student intake, the program managed to flourish. When it was introduced in 1989 there was one section of about 40 students. Today there are 135 students admitted each year.

The drive to develop new profiles and build on Lakeshore's unique foundation continued with the development of the Business Management profile in Financial Services. Nine of the program's 24 courses were co-developed with the Institute of Canadian Bankers (ICB) to be industry specific and highly specialized.

The new programs revitalized Lakeshore by helping it make the transition away from retraining. Then the College acquired the Lakeshore Psychiatric Facility and the possibilities became endless. The campus that once felt in the shadow of the North was about to take a giant step forward.

Built in 1890, the old psychiatric hospital was comprised of a central building and several cottages forming a quadrangle. The addition of this historic site to the campus meant the undertaking of a multi-million dollar restoration project.

The first cottages were finally opened in 1996. The following year, Michael Hatton was appointed Dean and the business programs at the North and Lakeshore campuses were united. With strong leadership and more space, the Lakeshore campus Business School really came into its own.

In 1997, the Human Resources, International Marketing and Marketing Management postgraduate programs moved to Lakeshore from the North. It was the first time in Humber's history that existing programs were relocated. Today all the Business School's postgraduate programs are clustered within the old residential cottages where students enjoy an environment similar to that of an established old university.

Lakeshore began to experience growth at a phenomenal pace. In 1999, the new International Project Management postgraduate program was launched at Lakeshore. Since the campus was now fully developed and able to support year-round activity, 12-month programs were offered, starting with International Project Management. Then came Public Administration. In the fall of 2002, the Professional Golf Management postgraduate program moved from the North. The same year, two more Cottages were opened. With even more space available, the three-year Golf Management program was moved.

"Now it's a big business campus with tremendous variety," says Meek. "Back in 1981 it was essentially a retraining centre, but in 20 years there's been a big shift. Today there is a range of skills being taught here."

Michael Hatton tells us that programming at Lakeshore took off beyond expectation. In fact, it even went beyond the country's borders.

"In the nineties, the Business School at Lakeshore campus embarked on a variety of international partnerships, all internationally funded, with great success."

First up was a four-year partnership project with a management training organization in Bangladesh called MIDAS – Micro Industries Development Assistance Society. Next came a four-year project with the Ministry of Education in Guyana to improve technical and business opportunities at the post-secondary level.

"And since the unification of the business programs at Lakeshore and the North, we're just now completing a four-year project with Zimbabwe, which, in spite of the challenges that country faces, has been an extremely successful project in terms of improving life opportunities for the poor, particularly women and youth, by infusing entrepreneurial education into technical training programs. That particular program has been led by faculty in Humber's Business School who have expertise in

entrepreneurial training methods."

Adds Dean Hatton, "We now have a bid in on a similar project in Tanzania."

While the Lakeshore campus has had a string of success stories, they've also had one notable false start. In 1999, a 12-month postgraduate program in Direct Marketing was developed but ran only one year.

"It seemed like such a good idea," says Meek. "We had employers lined up for graduates but we couldn't attract the students so we had to put it on hold."

As the evolution of the Lakeshore campus continues, the focus will be on the development of applied degrees and postgraduate programs. It couldn't be more different from the campus it once was.

"Now there's a feeling here that's more like a university," says Meek. "It's still very different from the North campus, but its difference is its strength."

Chapter 4
THE 90s: CONSOLIDATION

Chapter 4 | The 90s: Consolidation

The achievements of an organization are the results of the combined effort of each individual

VINCENT LOMBARDI

The dawn of the nineties sees a tumultuous time. Leadership is an issue, it seems, from the start of the decade until Michael Hatton's appointment as Dean in 1997. The School was wrought with cutbacks and setbacks. Morale was lower than it had ever been and at times disheartened faculty questioned administration's commitment to what was still the biggest School in the College.

It begins in 1990, with Dean Jack Buckley's resignation as he accepts the position of President at a college in Nova Scotia. Buckley had offered the Business School a sound

management style under which many staff and faculty members thrived. Yet during his tenure there was growing dissent from faculty members who believed that the Dean should have a strong background in business, unlike Buckley who, before coming to the Business School, worked his way through the ranks in the Health Sciences Division to become Dean.

So many saw his departure as an opportunity to find a leader with a breadth of practical business experience. A national competition was held to fill the position and in 1991 Lloyd Rintoul was appointed Dean. He had acquired extensive business experience with major corporations such as Moore Systems and Rockwell, and was reputed to be good at implementing change.

His success in the private sector boded well for the School. But without experience in a college culture

or working with unions, he seemed unprepared for the realities of life at Humber.

At the time, the predominant business philosophy in the manufacturing sector was Total Quality Management (TQM) – revising and enhancing every process in order to improve quality. With Rintoul behind the wheel, TQM became a focus for the School.

Establishing TQM was a bumpy road. The problem, as was typical for Rintoul, was working with the faculty. John Riccio, then Chair of Marketing programs reporting to Rintoul, remembers the Continuous Improvement Meeting to introduce the TQM process to the School.

"He decided he'd have a meeting of all faculty on Friday afternoon at 4:30," says Riccio. "He wouldn't take any excuses for people not coming. He put a memo out and received notes from people trying to get out of it. But he wouldn't accept them –

he'd just send the notes back. So the big splash introduction started with a number of people being upset with the process. Some people didn't show up – maybe in protest at the scheduling – and Rintoul was very angry."

"But he was great with numbers," adds Riccio. "When it came to budgets, he exposed a lot of problems with the School's processes. And when he left I used some of the ideas he had implemented."

For Michael Hatton, Chair of Business and Assistant Principal at Lakeshore campus from 1990 to 1994, Rintoul's determination to initiate TQM at the North meant Lakeshore could operate more freely.

"There was a lot of internal focus on things at the North. As a result, one saw significant change and growth in Lakeshore programs at that time," says Hatton.

"During that period we reduced the number of programs at Lakeshore by half and doubled the enrollment. It made the business programs at Lakeshore self-supporting. Before that we were running very niche-oriented programs with very small student numbers in senior years – less than ten in some cases – which put the question of viability at Lakeshore on the table."

"But by consolidating the programs with fewer options and strengthening the curriculum in multiple entry sections we had at least one solid section in the senior year. We ensured that business programming would not only stay at Lakeshore but would grow and develop. And it is still the major programming unit at Lakeshore."

The emphasis on international

According to Laurie Turner, Business Administration Coordinator, Rintoul made two important contributions to the Business School: TQM and international

partnerships. He aggressively promoted the School's "world class education" to universities around the world.

"He encouraged everyone to create international partnerships," says Turner. "So there was a flurry of activity as everyone took trips to places like Mexico, Germany and France to arrange agreements with institutions all over the world. Many of the initiatives ended with Rintoul's departure – although in the late nineties Michael Hatton, then Dean, received a call from a university in Chihuahua, Mexico, saying 'The 25 students are ready to come,' calling in on a long-forgotten agreement that was made in the Rintoul years. These students were supposed to do the third year of a business program at the Business School as part of an exchange, but we didn't have any students wanting to go to Chihuahua. And they had students for the next three years who wanted to take advantage of the exchange."

Lyon, France

Program Coordinator Mike Planche, (right) in Tanzania

Students are still coming to the Business School from that Mexican university. Today, though, they're paying international student fees.

In the early days of international exchange agreements, Turner arranged for two students to be exchanged each year with Université Claude-Bernard in Lyon, France – an arrangement which continues to this day. While it's easy to find students interested in coming to Canada, it's more difficult to find Business School students willing to learn overseas.

"Our students are very focused," says Turner. "They want to get on with life, get a job and an income. But we'll continue to host students from France even when we have fewer to send because these are fabulous students. You can get a lot from them – they raise our profile. It's a nice flavour for the Business School."

John Riccio tells us of another program developed during the Rintoul years. A partnership of the Canadian and German governments, it was an exchange program based on the German system of studying for six months and working for six months in a paid co-op. The program was a great success with students both overseas and at Humber. But, as classes grew, the Business School found it increasingly expensive to find field placements for visiting German students, and the program was no longer feasible when the Germans decided that they would not provide financial support.

Rintoul leaves

There are few details of Rintoul's departure from the Business School. "Lloyd left Humber after a relatively short term," says Richard Hook, Vice President Academic. "Just as most private sector companies have tried and rejected the concept of the 'learning organization', any move from a hierarchical profit-driven organization into a college comes with a potential conflict of values. My sense is that a difference of values was at the root of his departure from Humber."

In the year after Buckley left, before Rintoul became Dean, no one was at the helm. To deal with the lack of leadership, the four Chairs of the Business School and the Director of the Centre for Employee Benefits formed what was referred to as "Dean in a Team."

The Team functioned as Dean by creating a forum for all the Chairs to raise issues and make decisions. Their excellent rapport and many years working together made it a relatively easy management process. While the Business School had no representation in top-level College meetings, the "Dean in a Team" kept the Business School running smoothly.

With Rintoul's departure in March, 1993, the Team was called upon again to manage the School.

"It was incredible," says Laurie Turner. "Under Rintoul the Chairs grew closer and formed a strong, supportive team. When he left, there was a close knit and experienced group to take over."

"They ran the School without status, but they did it. They were great people who communicated well. I was once in a meeting with these five guys and I noticed how they all complemented one another. I remember thinking 'this is a team.'"

"Then," says Turner, "the reorganization came and blasted it apart."

And then there were two

In 1994, the College was reinvented as President Gordon modified the academic structure. Now, instead of being comprised of five large academic divisions, the College was made up of ten Schools.

The Technology division was broken into several Schools, the Media School emerged from creative arts, and Hospitality and Tourism became its own School. At the Business School, Accounting and Information Technology were spun off into a separate School, the Dean of which was John Liphardt, former Dean of the Business School.

"The idea behind that separation was that smaller units would be more nimble; more functional. But there was also the potential to develop accounting on the basis of a strong information technology underpinning," says Michael Hatton.

As technology was playing a more significant role in accounting, it was thought a marriage between IT and accounting would benefit both. The belief was that Humber could become a leader in the New Accounting by allowing it to evolve on its own. To this day, Accounting and IT remain separate from the Business School.

Aside from losing two large programs, the Business School took a big loss in human power. The "Dean in a

Team" was no longer able to function since Chair Dave Haisell returned to faculty, Chair Ken Simon went to the newly-formed School of Manufacturing, and Ted Patterson moved to BISC with the Centre for Employee Benefits. The loss of the Centre for Employee Benefits continues to disadvantage the Business School students and faculty.

The two remaining Chairs – Toby Fletcher and John Riccio – were appointed School Heads. This title, conferred by administration, was to be the beginning of a trend to replace the title "Dean" throughout the College. But it never caught on.

"We reported to the Vice President Academic," says Riccio. "But without the title of 'Dean' we weren't recognized as such by faculty. Really, the Dean structure is essential because without it you don't have the same power base."

As the smoke cleared from the reorganization, Fletcher and Riccio held a

John Riccio, (right) with a group of Business Administration students

faculty retreat. Since both had management training it seemed a logical step.

"John and I genuinely wanted to consult with faculty, listen to their concerns, and explain the College's financial challenges, especially how the impending cuts would affect the Business School," says Fletcher. "Prior to any cuts, one of the major issues involved significant disruption

to curriculum and, therefore, to students because the computer faculty now reported outside the Business School, but their offices remained in our area. The accounting faculty remained in F221, seemingly at a distance, and also had their reportability changed. It posed a morale challenge because the accounting courses and teachers were so deeply

Office Administration faculty help celebrate Shirley Harrison's (front middle) retirement

integrated into all the business curriculum that it was difficult to implement some of the required changes."

"We chose an experienced facilitator, Paul Tremlett, and he ran a very open two days of problem-identification and problem-solving workshops. At every opportunity, John and I expressed our views and tried to clearly indicate how we were going to co-manage and what we planned to do."

Along with the reorganization came an edict that the Business School reduce its expenditures by 15 percent. On very short notice, Fletcher and Riccio had to terminate the contracts of a significant number of part-time, partial load and sessional teachers.

"John and I immediately organized faculty meetings by program to initiate discussions on cutting curriculum hours, a very contentious issue as you can imagine, but the only way to realize the required 15 percent cuts."

"Of course everyone was affected one way or another and some were not at all happy with the results; however, we kept moving, consulting and adapting."

But Riccio explains that the cutbacks were made even more difficult by the fact that when accounting and IT left the School, their budgets went with them – even though many business programs still relied heavily on accounting and IT courses.

"So we had to pay other Schools for those courses," says Riccio. "It cost about 55 percent of our budget. We kept being asked to be efficient but we only really controlled half of our budget. As a result we didn't have a lot of leeway. Our argument was that money should come back, but after the reorganization the College didn't want to ruffle feathers." In fact, one of the first things Michael Hatton did when he took over as Dean in 1997, was to ensure the Business School was responsible for its own course delivery, exclusive of

communications and general education.

Says Laurie Turner about the events of 1994, "Everything was stretched to its limits. It was brutal downsizing and it left a bad feeling in the Business School. We lost accounting and information technology, we lost Chairs, we lost part-timers, and everyone had to do more work. And to top it off there was no Dean."

"It was bad for morale. Rumours were rife that the Business School would be split or that there wouldn't be a Business School, that we'd just become a business service course provider for other Schools. A couple of emotional memos went to the President's Office. The feeling was that the future of the Business School was uncertain. There was nobody to speak for us — nobody to defend us."

Says Fletcher, "I was seen as Chair and the only administrator for 50 full-time staff, 60 part-time staff and 60 evening school faculty. There was a two-year period where I had to go to 14 advisory board meetings and worked every evening for Continuing Education."

"Fortunately, I had great coordinators, people on whom we could rely. The Business Manager, Nancy Pearce, was terrific. She knew all the budget ins and outs."

"But it had to erode. The breadth was just too much. There was always the horrible feeling that disaster was about to happen."

"We made a lot of tough decisions," says Fletcher about the four long years the Business School ran without a Dean. "They were very unpopular. Yet we struggled to maintain curriculum, integrity, and credibility."

In 1996, Riccio became ill and went on sick leave for six months. Once again, Richard Hook, Vice President Academic, took a leadership role in the Business School. (In 1986, Hook covered for John Liphardt when he went on sabbatical for a year, but times had changed

dramatically since then.)

"Several things had changed in the intervening years," says Hook. "First, after a shift in administrators, there was some lack of strategic continuity. This is not a criticism of anyone, but is the inevitable result of so many changes."

"Second is the fact that the College had now faced a number of years of budget cuts (years in which the funding unit per student actually declined). The increasing challenges of how to share scarce resources and the perception that 'things were now worse than before' worked against morale. The same thing occurred in each School in the College but some were able to weather the conflict more easily through established and stable relationships."

"Third, the School was, at that time, on the edge of a significant number of retirements — a time when the faculty (many of whom had worked with their colleagues since the early years of the College) were now leaving the

College and being replaced by newcomers. The result was a dislocation of long-standing teams, the loss of comfortable relationships and the introduction of new human and academic dynamics."

"Quite frankly, the commitment of faculty to high academic standards, to being an outstanding business school, to actively participating in international learning opportunities remained unchanged. But the School needed stability."

Throughout the years that the School Heads were leading the Business School, the faculty consistently complained to administration about the lack of an official Dean. As a result, the President's Office commissioned a review of the School. The outcome was that, in 1997, Michael Hatton was appointed Dean.

Says Hook, "An external review of the school was implemented and a decision was taken to provide stable leadership and a chance to 'regroup.'"

When John Riccio returned after sick leave, he returned to his first love, full-time teaching.

Deans or not, the innovations continue

Perhaps the most incredible aspect of those years between Deans was that it was a highly innovative and productive time.

Says Fletcher, "Both John and I agreed to maintain, as best we could, all the activities we felt were strategic to the Business School's future success – most notably our international initiatives, partnerships with universities, new programs, and new delivery methods."

New staff were developed and new initiatives took off. For instance, a new e-Commerce profile was developed for the Business Administration program. Way ahead of its time, the e-Commerce profile evolved to become the e-Business degree program offered through the Business School as of fall 2003.

And the Business School led the way in championing a variety of cutting-edge delivery methods.

Says Riccio, "We developed a CD-ROM for an online marketing course and online learning packages for the Legal Assistant program. We were one of the first Schools in the College to look at using technology in the classroom."

He adds, "But the biggest thing we did was try to feel like a school again. People felt decimated. We weren't the same as we used to be before the reorganization."

So the business of education went on. Toby Fletcher continued working diligently with John Murray to find opportunities to allow students to complete degrees at universities.

"My impression is that the vast majority of students had not considered a degree until they came to the Business School and started getting excited about learning," says Fletcher. "We focused on Business Administration students because they were asking for it."

While transfer agreements with York and Ryerson were established in the eighties, Fletcher was now looking to broaden the scope. As credentialism flourished and more faculty members who joined the Business School came with impressive academic credentials, the time was right to push for degree completion opportunities for students.

"We were getting feedback from places like Ryerson saying our students were very well prepared," he says. "So it was clear that we were well positioned to focus on degrees. I began going out to universities trying to arrange local partnerships while John Riccio was doing the same thing internationally."

In 1993, Fletcher explored possibilities with the University of Guelph, University of Waterloo and Wilfrid Laurier. At Wilfrid Laurier he met Dr. David Murray, Dean of Business, and the two struck up a friendship that led to partnership opportunities. They worked on a very innovative Masters of Business Administration program geared to the Business School's Human Resources postgraduate students. Fletcher secured a 25 percent advanced standing for grads of the HR postgraduate program who wished to complete an MBA.

"It was an ideal arrangement because Wilfrid Laurier was looking for a foothold in the GTA," says Fletcher.

Called "Laurier on the Lake", since it was offered at our Lakeshore campus, the program was created with the full support of President Gordon and Lorna Marsden, then the President of Wilfrid Laurier University. While the program ran quite successfully for a short time, it ceased to operate in 1998 when Marsden moved to York.

During the same year, Fletcher met Michael Nightingale, Director of the School of Hospitality at the University of Guelph. His friendship with Nightingale proved beneficial in later years when Nightingale became Assistant Vice-President (Academic) of Guelph University. He was particularly supportive of a college/university partnership that blossomed into the University of Guelph-Humber, now located at the North campus.

The desire for partnerships with universities reflected a growing shift in the priorities of our students – and employers. In an effort to maximize both theoretical and applied education, many of Ontario's business students began attending both college and university. The combination of degree and diploma was increasingly seen as the ideal preparation for the modern workplace.

"Back in the early days, universities and colleges didn't talk," says Laurie Turner. "Now in the Business Administration program, 30 percent of grads go on to university and get advanced standing – that's evolution. Students realize the workplace is looking for degrees."

"Plus, creating transfer agreements was an important strategic move for the Business School. The agreements were validation; proof that what we were offering was at the degree level. When it came time to approach the government about creating our own degree programs, we could demonstrate that universities saw us as peers."

The mid-nineties were also important years for the development of distance education. Seneca and Humber created a consortium with three other colleges in order to offer basic business education at a distance. The idea was that if each college produced one course, all five colleges would be able to offer a complete program.

That early program became the basis for the development of a range of distance education options in the Business School. Currently, most courses in our two-year Business Management program can be studied through distance education. And so can the entire Human Resources

Management certificate and the Professional Sales certificate.

"As well as traditional book-based distance education, more and more of these courses are incorporating new technologies," says Alvina Cassiani, Associate Dean at the North Campus since 2002, and Director of Professional and Continuing Education prior to that.

"We simply can't believe the demand. We're working at a feverish pace to get more courses up and running. At the same time, we're examining new ways to use technology to make learning off campus even more dynamic."

Programs without funding

Another innovation of the mid-nineties was fee-for-service programs – programs that were not government funded but financed entirely by student tuition. Two of these programs were the Professional Golf Management program and the Flight and Aviation Management program. The

success of these initiatives was based on partnerships with professional associations.

"Lots of people were cynical," says Fletcher. "No one thought we'd get them up and running."

The Flight and Aviation program took off, so to speak, as soon as it was offered. The hands-on two-year profile of the Business Management program offered students business training coupled with flight training out of the Toronto Island Airport and, later, Brampton Airport. The program was phased out in 2000 in anticipation of a four-year degree program in this area.

The Professional Golf Management program is another story. Our partner – the Canadian Professional Golf Association (CPGA) – worked very well with the Business School and the result was a thriving program that literally had employers lined up for grads. In fact, the need for the program was successfully proven and today it receives government funding.

"The CPGA wanted the Business Administration credential for their professional golfers," says Fletcher. "They wanted them to be able to add value to the business side of golf. So they approached us with the idea for a program and we thought it was great."

"Toronto and Southern Ontario were the best places to start. We had clear indications that the golf industry was taking off, so it was ideal timing."

The Business School goes to China – again

In 1995, the President of Ningbo University in China approached the Business School. He was interested in establishing our flagship Business Administration program at their university – not a modified version, but one with an identical curriculum.

In China, at the time, there were few alternatives to a

Frank Franklin, Diane Simpson and Michael Hatton with graduates from Ningbo University

classical university education. But the growth in commercialization created a hunger for Western business practices and our Business Administration program seemed ideally suited to their needs.

"When the people from China came they'd done their homework," says Fletcher. "They wanted the type of education that made the Canadian economy so strong. They wanted software, marketing, sales, promotion and logistics curricula – the exact areas where the Business School was excelling."

So faculty members once again packed up and headed to China – but this time to teach university students. The four-year program, created for Chinese students planning careers in international trade, consists of two years' study at Ningbo University followed by a year at the Business School, and an optional year available at several universities to complete the degree. Graduates receive a three-year diploma from Humber, and a degree if they continue on to year four.

The program was first offered in 1996, and two years later 12 Chinese students arrived at the Business School. The demand grew quickly as word spread about the unique Canadian program and the next year 26 students arrived, followed by 55 the following year.

While there are financial benefits for Humber – each student pays the international rate of $10,000 in year three – the ramifications of the project go beyond tuition fees.

"By doing this every year, it benefits the entire college community," says Frank Franklin, Chair of International Projects. "There are opportunities for our students to interact with Ningbo students on a day-to-day basis, learning about Chinese business and culture. The Chinese students go back to China with a keen knowledge of North American business practices and a network of friends and potential business partners."

"China is increasingly exporting to the world and trading possibilities for Canada are enormous. From Canada's point of view, the students from Ningbo are like ambassadors. They return to China with the knowledge that it is easy to do business with Canada. What this relationship does, in essence, is create important links for the future."

While everything about the program seems ideal today, the future of the program wasn't a sure thing.

Says Toby Fletcher, "When we started we didn't know we were successful until three years into it. And we had no idea what the immigration system would be like to work with. But, as it turns out, we broke new ground with Immigration Canada."

Fletcher says the agreement with Ningbo University was very strategic.

"It was professional development, curriculum development, student development. And because

Ningbo students were going to come here, it was strategic in that it was the beginning of a long-term relationship."

Always in business

Through the change in leadership, our connection with business and industry remained strong. In the 90s, a number of new programs were initiated to work more closely and directly with business.

In 1996, the Business School established the Centre for Excellence in Management Training. The concept of "centres of excellence" was taken up by the provincial government, which implemented centres to improve practices in the hospital sector, in business and in universities.

Recognizing that a key strength of the Business School was providing education in supervisory skills and management skills, we established a Centre for Excellence in Management Training geared to small business owners. The program focused on business plans, establishing loans, and other fundamentals of starting a small business.

At the Lakeshore, the business faculty worked with the Canadian Association of Bankers and the Government of Ontario to create a 20-hour "new start" training program for entrepreneurs wanting to get a government-backed start-up loan. Again, Humber was a leader in curriculum development.

Later in the decade, the Business School developed an innovative Bachelor's degree program for employees of Daimler-Chrysler.

"The company believed a more educated staff leads to a more profitable organization," says John Murray, the faculty member central to the program's development.

In order to provide a degree, a university partner was a necessity. Vice President Roy Giroux first tried to pull in Central Michigan University, but the program was of little interest to them.

The Open University of British Columbia, on the other hand, was downright enthusiastic.

A program was developed whereby Daimler-Chrysler employees who enrolled were given prior learning credit based on life experience. "One of the key elements of the program was that it saved time and money for students because of the prior learning assessment," says Murray. "And we delivered the courses at the Bramalea plant so students wouldn't have to drive to an institution after working a shift."

Almost 40 employees of Daimler-Chrysler went on to receive Bachelor's degrees. Says Murray: "When you look at these things they tell you a story. They tell you that Humber encourages creativity and innovation."

Ones that didn't fly

During the years without a Dean, several innovative academic programs were initiated but didn't take off.

They include: an alternative on-campus degree completion program; the Canadian Management Postgraduate program; the Training and Management Postgraduate program.

The Business School also experimented with a variety of timetabling models. In order to maximize space and meet the needs of a student population that was increasingly juggling home and employment responsibilities along with college, the School offered students a choice of morning or afternoon classes.

The concept didn't work, though, because an imbalance of students always wanted a morning timetable and those who chose afternoons weren't fully committed to staying till late in the day. After trying it for two semesters, the model was abandoned.

Hatton arrives and stability returns

No member of the Business School staff or faculty would

dispute the fact that 1997 was a tough year. Tensions rose when the government announced 15 percent cutbacks across the community college system. Subsequently, the Business School was directed to ensure that program curricula averaged no more than 18 faculty contact hours per week.

All of the School's energy went into maintaining the quality of education with fewer teacher-student contact hours. And there was still no Dean.

Apparently, though, it wasn't for lack of trying.

"We ran through a bunch of candidates," President Robert Gordon explains. "Some very prominent people, I might add. But it became apparent they didn't really know much about Humber. We wasted time and the months went by with these searches. So we eventually arrived at the conclusion that the best solution was to get on with things because we were drifting."

"The solution was to take on someone who understands the College and had a business education, in this case an MBA. That's when Hatton went in there and things stabilized and we moved forward."

On April 1, 1997, in the midst of dramatic change, Michael Hatton was appointed Acting Dean. He had his job cut out for him. There hadn't been representation of the Business School at Dean level since 1993, and he'd inherited low staff and faculty morale along with serious budget constraints.

To make the context even more challenging, he continued in his former role as Dean of Media Studies. While he was appointed Dean of the Business School the following fall, it wasn't until January 1998 that he had fully wound down his duties at the Media School.

There were big issues to contend with right from the very beginning. When

he first arrived, the Business School was grappling with the decision of whether or not to move the Human Resources, International Marketing, and Marketing Management postgraduate programs to the Lakeshore Campus.

"There had been issues in terms of student satisfaction and resources in those programs," says Dean Hatton. "There was a lot of related discussion and debate during the April, May, June period. Faculty wanted to be sure they had a forum to shape and direct their vision about where their programs were going. We came out with several themes, and these included confirming the move of programs to Lakeshore and facilitating those as best as possible."

Moving the postgraduate programs was only the beginning of the major decisions made in Hatton's early days.

"A second element was working to shift the faculty orientation to a more

program-based perspective rather than a discipline-based perspective, particularly at the diploma level. In large part this was based on the view I hold that the program is our product. Students aren't coming here to study specific disciplines, they're here to get diplomas. To my mind, that shift was very important."

"And, of course, it was essential to involve faculty directly in that process because at the heart of what we offer is the faculty who deliver our programs. If that's tangible from the student perspective the value rises dramatically and the marketing of everything is much easier."

"Another element we looked at closely at that time is how well we market our programs. Most critical, we looked at the messages from the students' perspective, and that continues to be our evaluative focus."

When Hatton was initially appointed Acting Dean in April 1997, his mandate was to identify and report on issues and recommend the appropriate courses of action to the President. One of the issues he identified was that the School's flagship programs – Business Administration and Business Management, the programs that enroll the bulk of business students – didn't necessarily have the appropriate curriculum for the latter part of the nineties. Or, at a minimum, the curriculum had not been validated for many years. Also, he brought to light the fact that the Marketing program was attracting fewer and fewer applicants, thereby emphasizing the need for renewal.

So in early 1998, a major review of the curriculum was kicked off, spearheaded primarily by the Planning Department of Humber College. They worked through a variety of Human Resources Development Canada (HRDC) reports on employment data, interviewed employers, spoke to faculty, and reviewed curricula from colleges and universities across Canada.

"They came up with a series of recommendations which were hotly and appropriately debated the length and breadth of the Business School," says Hatton. "They made suggestions about courses and the orientation of programs in order to maximize the potential for students, the benefits for employers and opportunities for further study."

One of their recommendations was a common first year for Business Management, Business Administration and Marketing, so students could change programs after the first year. Although a common first year was implemented in the late eighties, it had eroded over time.

"A key recommendation from that review was that the three-year Business Administration program should be geared toward our highest-level students in order to maximize their potential for transferring to university. And, after the common first year, the two-year Business Management program should focus on course work that would maximize the potential for job readiness."

"It was thought that the Marketing program should be similar in thrust to Business Management, except with a strong orientation to the marketing discipline. After implementing those changes, which was no mean feat, we then recast all of our promotional material and started promoting ourselves on the basis of that material." And to this day, Hatton continues to make significant inroads in the marketing of the Business School, with the creation of unique promotional materials, including a variety of brochures, posters and the Business School's magazine, *Connections*.

Another bone of contention in 1997 – as it had been since the eighties – was the separation of the business programs at the Lakeshore and North campuses. After nearly three decades of inconsistency and shifting accountability, faculty had had enough.

Hatton included in his report to the President the recommendation that the programs be united — and Dr. Gordon agreed. The change was to be implemented over the course of the next academic year.

Come winter 1998, Pat Ferbyack, who was responsible for the business programs at the original Lakeshore site and Ian Smith, who was responsible for the business programs in the Cottages of the Robert A. Gordon Learning Centre (formerly the Lakeshore Psychiatric site) would, for the academic purposes of those programs, work through the Dean of Business at the North campus. The following summer, Pat Meek was selected as Chair of Business at the Lakeshore campus responsible for the diploma and postgraduate programs, including the programs in both the old Lakeshore building and the restored buildings. Toby Fletcher continued as Chair of Business programs at the North.

"So now we had a Chair at the North, a Chair at Lakeshore and a single Dean," says Hatton. "Interestingly enough, that's probably the leanest administrative structure at the North campus since the sixties. By contrast, in the early nineties there were five Chairs in the Business School at the North, a Dean, as well as a Business Chair at Lakeshore who reported to the Principal of Lakeshore."

Hatton made another significant recommendation to the President. He requested that Accounting be considered for reintegration back into the Business School.

That was not to happen.

One office fits all

Another ongoing issue for the Business School was office space. There's never been enough.

When the North campus opened in 1968, all Humber's faculty members were housed where the President's Office is today. As the divisions grew, faculty began to cluster by area of expertise in various areas throughout the College.

The business curricula of the seventies, however, drew faculty from a variety of disciplines, so business offices sprang up around the entire College. Come the eighties, the Business School functioned from ten different offices on three floors, not including Lakeshore.

And the location of the central office wasn't always optimal. Through the seventies and most of the eighties, it was where the bookstore is today. However, when a College redesign required a new location, the Business School found itself in a much less desirable spot in E building, where it is currently located. But the main entrance was down a dark hallway adjacent to the elevator entrance. For that entire period it was very difficult for students to find the Business School. And because it wasn't large enough to house all the faculty it spawned nodes of faculty groupings spread throughout the institution.

At that time, before the reorganization of 1994, if you had gathered all the programming that contained business components, it would have comprised half the teaching activity at the College. The space simply was not available to house all business programming in one spot.

When Hatton arrived, though, Accounting, Information Technology and the Centre for Employee Benefits had left the School. Plus, over the years there'd been a slow transition from a primary emphasis on full-time staff and a few part-timers to a faculty composition that included many more part-time specialists. The size was now more manageable and unification was finally possible.

Hatton had the central office renovated, complete with a highly accessible new entrance. The design allowed for all the program coordinators and staff to be housed under the same roof.

"There was finally a sense of affiliation," says Laurie Turner. "We started to feel connected. And I think that has been a real strength of the Business School since Michael [Hatton] arrived. Now we're all aware of what the others are doing and how we affect one another."

As the nineties drew to a close, the Business School was smaller but, in many ways, it was more focused and much stronger. The changes implemented by Dean Hatton began to quell the anxieties of staff and faculty. It seemed that, at last, the Business School had the leadership it needed to move confidently into the next millennium.

Chapter 5
2000 TO 2003 AND BEYOND:
NEW PATHWAYS

Chapter 5 | 2000 to 2003 and beyond: New Pathways

Do not go where the path may lead, go instead where there is no path and leave a trail.

RALPH WALDO EMERSON

The 21st century began with a bang. All the necessary pieces were in place for the Business School to position itself as a serious senior player in Ontario's post-secondary educational environment and attract some of the province's brightest and best students. The positive mood was fuelled by bold initiatives that would, by their very nature, separate the Business School from the pack.

Provincially, the government was anticipating the double cohort – the year when the number of students graduating from high school would be doubled due to the elimination of Ontario Advanced Credits (OACs). In addition, demographic studies anticipated strong growth in the 20-24 year old population within the GTA for the next five to seven years. In preparation, the government provided funds for the growth of post-secondary institutions.

The timing was fortuitous. The Business School was able to push forward with a number of key initiatives that will benefit students long after the infamous double cohort year. When that wave of students arrives, the Business School will be ready. According to Dean Michael Hatton, the School will be central to managing the issue for the entire College.

"The Business School is probably the most flexible and responsive area within the College for a couple of reasons. One, the generic attraction of business programs is very strong among high school students since it doesn't have the same peaks and valleys as other areas in terms of attraction and job market. And by and large it's easier to grow in business than other areas, particularly compared to those that are lab dependent or require highly specialized resources."

"So in many respects the Business School is the double cohort catch basin. We first saw that in the 2002/2003 school year with the pre-shock of the fast-trackers trying to get ahead of the double cohorters."

"We've made a commitment to high schools that we will do our best to accommodate double cohort students in 2003 and 2004, and that includes continuing to develop relationships with follow-on institutions that allow students to continue their education immediately following Humber College or in later years."

Better by degrees

We'll also be ready with entirely new options in education.

In 2002, the Business School announced that it will offer two four-year degree programs, one in Paralegal Studies and the other in e-Business. And come 2005, there could be up to five applied degrees.

"The degrees have been the missing link," says Dean Hatton. "We offer certificates, diplomas and postgraduate certificates, but we've been missing degree programs."

Not only will the degrees be of immediate use to the industries they're designed to serve and to the students who take the programs, they elevate all the course offerings in the Business School. That may one day make it easier for students to get credit at more universities than is the present case.

"Colleges in this province generally have had difficulty doing justice to their students in terms of providing reasonable and appropriate degree completion opportunities," Hatton says.

"It's quite possible that within two to three years the opportunity for Humber to provide degrees will provide a resolution to that issue. Second, universities are becoming more competitive. Increasingly, they have to recognize that top performing college students are excellent university material and shouldn't be made to start programs from scratch. The fact that Humber will offer its own degrees will simply fuel that evolution."

Dr. Robert A. Gordon, President of Humber College, believes the four-year degrees are the result of a new societal demand.

"We're not adding degrees because we think it's more prestigious, but because we believe the changing world is requiring a different type of person who needs advanced credentials which have become a factor in the 21st century," says Gordon. "These credentials weren't a factor after the Second World War. During that period people were mulling over the creation of the college system to create a middle-level infrastructure for a society that was post-industrial. It was a great innovation, but the point they left out was the individual's aspiration to move forward. So there's a mismatch, and the individual gets frustrated."

"What we're trying to do is provide opportunities for our students so that it's possible to continue their education if they wish to go on."

"Increasingly, we have data that suggests students want a bachelor's degree when they enter Humber. Five years ago it was a very low percentage, now well over 70 percent of our freshman are saying they have every intention of completing a bachelor's degree. Primarily, we're creating opportunities for our students to have access to a number of pathways, ideally that are linked together."

"The Business School is particularly important," he says. "Other disciplines come and go but business is fundamental. There are probably more people in our society that foresee they'll be in a business career as opposed to other careers and, therefore, the unlimited potential is greatest."

Our new degree programs help the Business School fulfill new needs created by industry. And, from the beginning, that has been our purpose.

"We sold our degrees [to the government] on the grounds that it's hard for our students to transfer, and on the basis that the economy is not getting the kinds of graduates from the universities in many sectors that it needs. Paralegal is the classic example. Lawyers say that they need these kind of people doing the lower-level legal work, but no one else offers this degree."

Dr. Gordon adds that

the double cohort has been a blessing for Humber.

"The beauty of the double cohort and the expansion of this demographic group in the GTA is that we're able to add another layer onto our programming without disrupting what we were already doing."

"Our degrees have little to do with the double cohort, they have more to do with the global economy, the way the world is moving and the needs of individuals to have upgraded credentials. They coincidentally came at the same time as the double cohort, which allowed us to have significant growth painlessly."

The new degrees will be available at the Business School as of fall 2003. While students applying to these programs must meet typical university entrance requirements, they can expect an education that's a hybrid of university and college. They'll receive a broad spectrum of theory, but they'll also be treated to a thorough agenda of practice, including work terms.

Developed and evaluated by a team of law professionals, the one-of-a-kind Paralegal Studies degree will change the nature of legal education in the country.

"With a BAA, our graduates will have so many options," says Philip Sworden, Coordinator of the Court and Tribunal Agent program, who helped develop the new degree. "They'll be able to apply to law school if they choose, or to the University of Toronto's Centre of Criminology. And, of course, they'll be well equipped to enter the paralegal field right away."

Paralegals are often an alternative to lawyers, performing important advocacy services for clients appearing before specialized boards and tribunals such as the Ontario Rental Housing Tribunal and the Ontario Small Claims Court. The need for paralegals is growing as our society becomes more open to airing its problems in court – and as the cost of lawyers' services increases.

"While the disputes and dollar amounts may not justify the cost of a lawyer, they still require proper, efficient representation," says Sworden. "Paralegals are the ideal solution. They're affordable and they help ensure every citizen's access to justice."

"Paralegals have it made right now. They can choose to be self-employed or they can find work with established paralegal organizations, in corporate legal departments, in affiliation with lawyers as researchers, collection agents, investigators, or with courts and tribunals. The time is right for this degree."

And the Business School is the logical place for it. Current faculty members are skilled lawyers by background, and some are judges. What's more, our program and graduates have a strong reputation in the field. Both the Law Clerk and Court and Tribunal Agent programs are well known and respected in the legal community.

The e-Business degree is another important step for industry. Developed to meet a need expressed by industry for employees with the right combination of business knowledge and a comprehensive grasp of the tools and practices of e-business, our new degree is unlike anything offered elsewhere.

And it's just in time. e-business has already revolutionized the way in which business is conducted. More than one out of every 10 companies uses the Internet to sell goods and services, with global Internet commerce expected to exceed $3.9 trillion Canadian by 2004.

"The e-Business degree is unique because from the start of the four-year program, students will be exposed to university-level concepts in the classroom, which will be concurrent to exposure in the laboratory with software and tools that form the basis of an applied education," says Edmund Baumann, Coordinator of the program.

Baumann tells us that the program is vital if Canadian businesses are to stay competitive in world markets. "The investment in e-business infrastructure at present delivers under one percent of all revenues generated by Canadian businesses. Going above that into the double digit range will take people trained in programs like this one."

The board of advisors for the development of the program consisted of both e-business solution suppliers, and e-business solution users. Some of the industry's best-known organizations were represented in the group. According to Baumann, all are committed to taking e-business students for the work term between the third and fourth year of the e-Business program. And that bodes very well for employment opportunities following graduation.

The University of Guelph-Humber arrives

As the new century dawned, credentialism at the Business School was in full bloom. Now most students were arriving here with plans to complete university degrees – and that's because most employers began to see the combination of practice and theory as the ideal preparation for the modern workforce.

For students, though, the process of acquiring a diploma and a degree was expensive and time consuming. It could take up to six years to complete.

By way of a solution, Humber College joined forces with the University of Guelph to launch the University of Guelph-Humber. As of fall 2002, the new university offered several degree programs, each of which has a base in academic theory as well as a focus on experiential learning through strong linkages with employers. To house the venture, an impressive new facility was created at Humber's North campus.

One of the first programs out of the gate was the Bachelor of Business Administration program. An eight-semester, four-year program leading to an honours degree, it allows a projected intake of 300 students per year to specialize in one of five areas: marketing, international business, finance, management of not-for-profit enterprises, and small business/entrepreneurship.

Dean Hatton says the program is particularly beneficial to students who thought they'd have to leave Toronto to earn an applied degree.

"Now local students can complete an applied BBA program without a major move. Here they get the practical learning for which we're so well known, combined with the commerce and theoretical perspectives for which the University of Guelph is held in high esteem. As well, the program leads to a degree with the option of postgraduate study at graduation or later on, in the shortest time possible."

While there were clear advantages for business students, who until now had to choose between leaving town or spending additional years in school to get this education, there were advantages for the Business School, too. The new BBA program strengthened our position in the marketplace.

"The Business School offers one of the broadest ranges of programming options available at any business school in Canada," says Dean Hatton. "This degree simply increases that range of programming, and that benefits both our current students and our new students."

The dynamic union of educational styles – one

Artist's concept sketch of the new Guelph-Humber building

Building Business A History of the Business School at Humber

that's steeped in generations of academic tradition and another that changes with shifts in the winds of employment – is a learning experience in itself.

"We're learning a great deal from Guelph. In all our programming, we believe we have as much to learn as we have to teach. That's what keeps us fresh and on the edge: our commitment to learning," says Hatton.

Michael Nightingale is responsible for the University of Guelph's role in the project. He had been waiting for years for the opportunity to work with Humber on breaking some new ground in education.

"Humber and Guelph both have a reputation for being innovative," says Nightingale, Assistant Vice-President (Academic). "Over the years we've explored a number of collaborative ventures but none came to fruition because of lack of funds for such initiatives."

"Then the government stepped in with some SuperBuild money to encourage collaboration and we saw it as an opportunity to put some plans into action. Since we were looking to do some growth off campus, the timing was ideal. We're excited by the idea of working together with Humber College," he says.

"At Guelph, we don't get as many students from Toronto as we'd like to, especially those who can't afford to study away from home. The growth of the market and the demand for post-secondary education is coming from the Toronto area, so this joint effort gives us much better reach."

The process of a college and a university coming together to create something new is a fascinating one. "We don't always agree," says Nightingale. "But that can be constructive tension. Thanks to this project, we're forced to take a new look at our objectives. Even in our own senate we're having discussions on this subject, we're forced to think more clearly about our role. We're re-examining the link between maintaining our standards and being on the frontier of education."

"It's a challenge bringing the culture of two organizations together. You have to find out how you work together. When we've had differences of opinion we've been able to put the project first so we're dealing with issues rather than protecting the status quo."

Construction of the Guelph-Humber building

"Whenever you get two different traditions coming together there's a synergy from which you get new ways of doing things," says Nightingale. "We're challenging different ideas – we're taking the best of both traditions."

The sound relationship that's been established lays the groundwork for bigger and better things. In fact, according to Dr. Gordon, President of Humber, the bachelor's degrees offered by the University of Guelph-Humber are only the beginning.

"We're working with Guelph on Masters degrees," says Dr. Gordon. "They're impressed with what we do. And because Guelph is so well known, it's a great place to start."

Postgraduate offerings are expanded

Of course, the double cohort will affect universities too – and that means that the need for postgraduate programs will grow in the latter part of the decade.

"Student growth presupposes new product offerings," says Dean Hatton. "We will offer more postgraduate programs because we realize university enrollments are growing and our postgraduate programs feed, for the most part, on generic university graduates. There will be tremendous opportunities in 2006, 2007 and 2008. We're the best-positioned college for postgraduate programs and we want to maintain, if not extend, that leadership."

The first new postgraduate program of the decade was the Public Administration program. Created as a result of a hiring boom within the government, the new program was launched in fall 2001.

During the early seventies, economic prosperity led to a hiring boom at all levels of Canadian government. But thirty years later, many of those public servants were ready for retirement. "Right now high-level positions are becoming vacant," says Ted Glenn, Coordinator of the Public Administration program. "The government is doing some leadership development to prepare middle management in public service for advancement. Everyone is moving up. There are a lot of entry-level jobs and many jobs to move up to."

The average age in Ontario's public service is 45. Less than three percent of employees are under 30 years old and 67 percent of public servants are between 40 and 60 years old.

But retirement isn't the only reason for the boom. In the early nineties the public service was 95,000 strong but today there are only 80,000 employees. Downsizing was the big culprit there, affecting the youngest and newest public servants – and worsening the impact of retirement.

Another influence is simply evolution. "There are changes to how programs are delivered, attempts to reduce red tape and a real effort to serve the public in a better way," says Glenn.

The combination of these factors has had an effect on more than just the quantity of jobs available. Today's public service positions are more varied than ever before.

And without a doubt the people filling the jobs are different than they were in the boom of the early seventies. Today's public servants are less homogenous and more interested in politics.

Says Glenn, "Students come here with undergraduate degrees in everything from history and anthropology to sociology and women's studies. They can use that background in the public service – all they need is an understanding of how the government works. And that's what the Public Administration program is all about."

Bonds with business get stronger

In the eighties, some faculty members were concerned that credentialism would interfere with the Business School's relationship with the business community. Twenty years later, that fear has been unfounded.

"The direct relationship with employers is very much a unique and important focus of the Business School," says Dean Hatton. "Employers drive our advisory committees which influence our programs in many different ways."

"And virtually all our programs offer breakfasts one or more times a year where students work directly with employers."

One of many Networking Breakfasts organized by The Business School

He's referring to the Networking Breakfasts held at both the North and Lakeshore campuses. Employers from a wide variety of businesses enjoy hot coffee and fresh croissants while searching for the next company superstar. At the same time, students have the chance to learn about a variety of business sectors – and convince employers that they're star material. But for many, it's simply a great opportunity to develop and refine networking skills.

The Networking Breakfasts have proven hugely popular with both employers and students. While it's informal, it's a potent way of drawing the business community closer to the Business School. Another innovative idea for keeping connected with employers is the Financial Services program's wine and cheese party. The crowning event of the final semester, the event

takes place, appropriately enough, in the corporate boardroom of a different big bank each year. It's attended by about 30 bankers, all of whom are prospective employers.

Hatton is so determined to maintain strong ties that he's taken the business of employer relationships to a whole new level. "We rely heavily on employers," he says. "So in 2001 we stepped outside tradition and hired two full-time people who do nothing but develop contacts between students and employers. There's one at North and one at Lakeshore."

And, in terms of student placements and fieldwork, the Business School is better situated than it ever was. Both students and employers are benefiting from a greater degree of hands-on experience. What makes it different today, though, is that students can take advantage of the practical component that colleges are known for without closing the doors on future educational options.

"In 2001, we finalized having a fieldwork component in every program. Employers see the need for that practical aspect of a college education," says Dean Hatton.

"At the same time, our students and our institution have matured, and there's an understanding that learning and education and certification is not going to stop with Humber College diplomas and certificates. We're not doing justice to students or faculty without the kinds of linkages with other institutions and our own higher-level programming. It gives our students and grads a chance to continue to accumulate knowledge, skills, attitudes, behaviours and the appropriate certification and recognition that goes along with that."

Developing beneficial partnerships

The Business School is also forging ahead in its relationships with professional organizations. In 2000, we established a relationship with the Canadian Professional Sales Association (CPSA).

Thanks to our partnership, the six courses necessary for designation can be taken as part of the Business Management and Marketing programs. Upon graduation, students may receive both a diploma from the Business School and a certificate of accreditation from the CPSA.

Once they become Canadian Sales Professionals with the letters "CSP" behind their names, the world knows they have the backing, the contacts and the prestige offered by the CPSA. And, significantly, employers know graduates have the fundamental skills, knowledge and attitudes needed for success in an entry-level sales position.

"For those business students who know they'll end up in sales, I see this certificate as an incredible opportunity," says Dean Hatton. "The advantage for them is that it indicates to prospective employers that they've had industry-vetted sales training. I think the industry is looking for credentials that are predictors of professionalism so it's very timely."

More recently, the Business School has developed a partnership with the Canadian Institute of Management, Canada's only management organization dedicated to professional development. Now as Business Administration students complete their program, they're also completing the necessary course work for the "CIM" designation.

"I think it comes down to credibility," says Joan Milne, executive director of the CIM. "We need to partner with credible colleges and Humber is offering the courses that prepare students not just for good business but for good business management. Graduates have the tools to do the job effectively and properly."

"Over 90 percent of people who are CIM certified say that there is a tangible benefit. With the designation, some get a higher salary, some get promotions, some get new business. Then there are the intangible benefits – how they feel because the designation recognizes their accomplishments."

Another partnership developed by the Business School resulted in a special partnership award signed by Prime Minister Jean Chrétien. At the request of the Federal Department of Justice, the Business School developed a customized two-year Law Clerk diploma. The program we created – the Ontario Regional Office Department of Justice Law Clerk Diploma program – is delivered on-site to government employees who wish to further their careers.

"Our goal is always to provide the education that's most relevant to employers," says Dean Hatton, who accepted the award on behalf of the Business School. "And this partnership gave us a chance to provide practical education for the purpose of upgrading skills to a whole new group of individuals."

He adds, "There's great potential in this relationship between Humber and the Department of Justice. I hope the future brings more opportunities to provide education to those who might not otherwise have the means to get it."

But the real strength of the program comes from the tremendous cooperation that exists between these two organizations. The program runs smoothly because the Business School and the Department of Justice share responsibilities, including administrative duties, registration, prior-learning assessment and even teaching.

Alvina Cassiani, Associate Dean of the Business School at the North Campus, tells us the program was so successful that a college in another province has requested help to start a similar program with the federal government.

"I'm not surprised," says Cassiani. "The program works very well. The students are happy, the Department is happy and the Business School is always pleased to find new ways to make education accessible."

"Empowering individuals with the knowledge they need to improve their lives – that's what it's all about. When employers recognize that it's in their best interest to help people grow, everybody wins."

The classroom metamorphosis

Of all the changes the Business School has seen over the years, one of the most profound is that of the students themselves. Of course, it can be argued that students are a product of their age. And there's no question – times have changed dramatically since the College opened its doors in 1967.

"Students have financial pressures now that they didn't have then," says Laurie Turner, Coordinator of the Business Administration program and a faculty member since the seventies. "In the late seventies it seemed that there was more money, especially for student loans and grants. Today students are much more likely to work part- or even full-time. There's a great number who are juggling studies and work because they have to earn a living. That wasn't the case then. And students today are consumers. They have greater expectations of service

Canadian Institute of Management, a Business School partner

and, in many ways, they're more demanding."

Ask any teacher – technology has had a huge impact on the classroom. Where students were once chided for talking during lectures, now faculty are more concerned about students using computers for instant messaging with their friends. They must remind students to turn their cell phones off. And they're expected to be available via e-mail as well as by phone and in person.

"Students have e-mail, voice-mail, and the Internet, so there are more ways to get information," says Turner. "They have an insatiable need for information. They can't seem to get enough."

Ken Simon taught at the Lakeshore campus in the seventies and early eighties. After moving through the ranks, as Program Coordinator, Chair of Business at North and Lakeshore and subsequently retiring as Associate Principal at Lakeshore, he's back to what attracted him to education in the first place — teaching.

"I taught at a time when the high school population coming to the College at the Lakeshore campus was quite small," says Simon. "This made for smaller classes and a more intimate group of students. Talk and chalk were the key methods of instruction with the occasional use of overheads and videotapes."

"Now that I am back in the classroom for some evening teaching, I find little difference in the students. However, if anything, the technology has made the classroom environment easier. The expectations and the delivery are more exciting. Communication techniques are more varied and interesting, and I believe that the students' expectations are somewhat higher."

"I find the use of e-mail and computers quite exciting.

Access to the Web makes student assignments more relevant and current. But the jury is still out on plagiarism."

According to Ross Richardson, who's been teaching marketing since the early eighties, class sizes have grown and that's had a less positive impact.

"I don't think we tend to be as close to students as we like because of the sheer class size."

Class make up is also very different. There was a day when the majority of students came directly from high school. "Many come from university, or they're graduate students so they're older and more experienced. They're not just out of grade 12," says Richardson.

"There's also a change in exposure to other cultures. Now English is a second language for many students in my classes. We're not community based any more, but I think it's a positive thing."

Where we're going

Thirty years later, the Business School is once again embracing tremendous growth – and with much the same passion we had in the seventies.

The increase in pathways offered by the Business School has been a major contributor to our growing numbers. In 1997, when Michael Hatton became Dean, the School had 2,500 students. By comparison, 3,200 students were registered for the 2002/2003 school year. And we will have up to 1,000 business students at the University of Guelph-Humber.

"The numbers will continue to increase dramatically over four to five years as our diploma programs continue to grow, as we increase the number of applied degrees and as we add to our postgraduate offerings," says Dean Hatton.

The addition of so many new programs has made hiring new faculty a necessity.

Indeed, more than one-third of the faculty members at the School in 2003 were not here in 1997.

"We're hiring at a rate that's unprecedented since the seventies. We now have the constant challenge of finding faculty members who match the calibre of what we've had in the past, and orienting them to the Humber culture. We're building on success so the orientation of new faculty is critical and, of course, time consuming."

The expansion of the Business School is part of a bigger story. Humber College is evolving at a brisk pace to meet the needs of a much broader student base. And, as it does, the School will continue to take advantage of the opportunities that are unfolding.

"We happen to be in a phase where we're growing," says Dr. Gordon. "There's obvious growth potential. We now have approval to offer even more degrees, up to 25, so we'll have a great

deal to offer at that level. People will start to realize that a degree from Humber is an extraordinarily valuable credential."

The growth in programming has necessitated physical change. In this decade, Humber College will start to look and feel very different.

"We're starting two new residences. We're also looking to expand Lakeshore, where we'll house a lot of business programs. Lakeshore will look like an Oxford quadrangle, a beautiful campus with residences, fitness facilities, a student centre, and a library. Students will be impressed," says Dr. Gordon.

"The Business School will be at both campuses. It's one of the few areas that is going to be big enough and programmatically diverse enough that it will actually pervade the two campuses."

Today, as yesterday, the pursuit of excellence

In 1967, a handful of students took a chance on a new type of business education offered temporarily in an old public school. The small classes, the faculty members who took an interest in them, and the job possibilities that awaited them when they graduated made the experience more satisfying than they perhaps thought education could be. Word spread. Graduating classes grew, creating a massive and expanding network of business people with a common bond – graduation from the Business School at Humber College.

Today enrollment is in the thousands, our program offerings include degrees and we compete for students with some of the country's finest business schools – but deep down, we're the same. We're still driven by genuine

enthusiasm and guided by a sincere belief in the value of what we have to offer. And today, as yesterday, there are no limits to what we can achieve.

Marching into the days and years ahead, our steps will be bold. We'll advance with the confidence that comes from a rich past and the vigour that comes with a worthy purpose. We'll do it for the employers who welcome our graduates, the students who are hungry for success, and the graduates whose accomplishments reflect so well on us.

The Business School continues to throw its heart and soul into the pursuit of excellence.

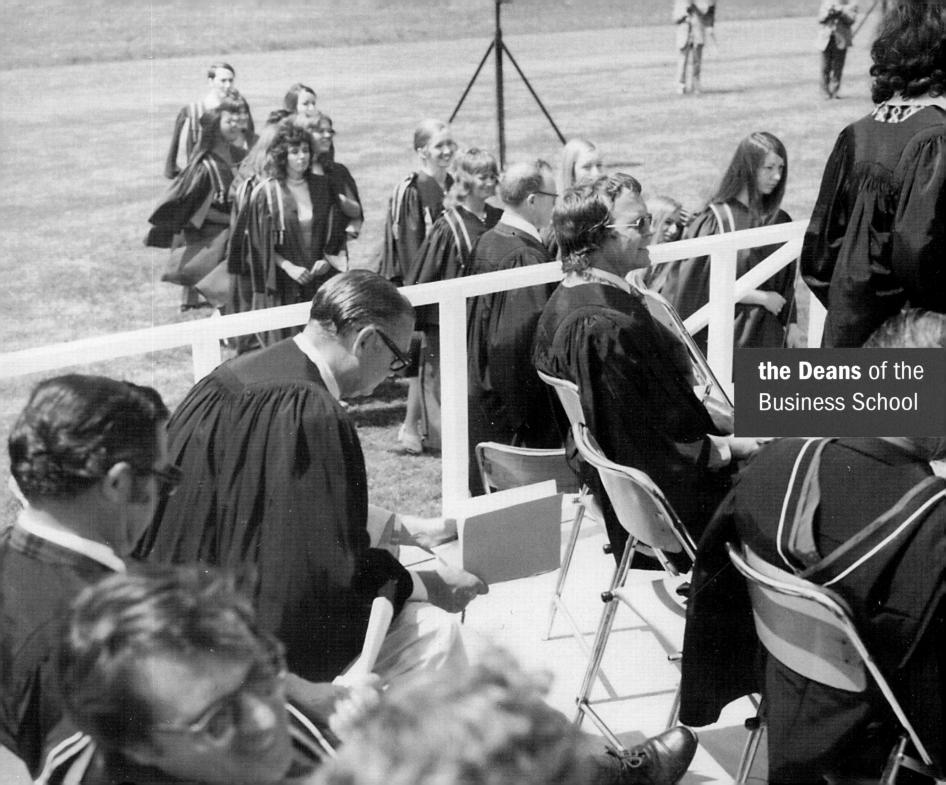

the **Deans** of the Business School

The Business School was fortunate to have a succession of committed deans who brought a wealth of vital skills to the job. In retrospect, it seems that each dean was particularly well suited to his era and had the talents necessary for that stage in the School's development.

A high school teacher and businessman before coming to Humber, John Almond was an entrepreneur by nature. As the School's first dean, his ability to build a winning enterprise from the ground up was crucial to early success.

"John Almond very quickly got business to recognize that the College existed," says Don Wheeler, who was hired by Almond in 1969. "He interacted with professional associations and went out and met with key players in industry. As a result, we had employers coming in very early. That was a real coup."

Wheeler remembers the numerous meetings that Almond set up with representatives from industry. And, more often than not, he brought a faculty member or chair with him to act as resident expert. The meetings not only kept the School connected with prospective employers, they helped in the development of program curricula.

Almond's astute hiring decisions had a profound effect on the future of the School. In fact, two of his "hires" became deans – and several more went on to become chairs. Most of the faculty members he hired came from senior management positions in industry. For Almond, the connection to industry was critical.

"He pushed the importance of consulting," says Wheeler. "He wanted staff current, and that meant being active in the field."

Yet he also worked very hard to develop rapport with faculty. "He was good at getting people on side. He used to include faculty in all meetings and ask their opinions. He built up morale. He was very precise and very business-minded, and he always treated people with respect."

Dean John Almond

Almond, who had an MBA from the University of Western Ontario, put a great deal of effort into developing the kinds of programs that would get students hired.

"As the first dean, he had to decide which programs to include – and to what academic level they should be developed. Every course in every program had to be scrutinized. And I believe he achieved his goal of offering programs that would develop highly marketable graduates."

While he experienced success on most fronts, many of those he worked with believe that Almond's greatest challenge may have been political. The Business School grew faster than other divisions at the College, so getting the appropriate funding always took tremendous rallying. By all reports the effort was, at times, frustrating.

In 1972, Almond received an offer to join Fact Photofinishing as general manager. After several years, he became executive vice president. With his usual entrepreneurial spirit, he was later involved in many businesses and worked extensively in the graphics industry.

One of Almond's early hiring decisions was Eric Mundinger, who worked at the family-run musical instrument business, Mundinger and Company, before coming to Humber. While Chair of Management programs in the Business School, Mundinger continued his education and was awarded a Masters of Education degree from OISE in 1971. The year Almond left he made a successful bid for the position of dean.

Mundinger really understood his environment and flourished in his new job. He knew how to make use of the system to get things accomplished. He was a strong administrator and ran a tight ship, all of which was increasingly important since the Business School was growing by leaps and bounds.

"His biggest challenge was the phenomenal growth," says Wheeler, who moved up from faculty and took over Mundinger's vacant chair position. "There was growth in faculty, growth in the student body and growth in job opportunities."

Adds Wheeler on the issue that would plague the School until 1997, "He kept trying to house the Business School in one area. In fact, the E building was constructed with the Business School in mind, but then the Health Sciences division was created in the seventies and took over the fourth floor and part of the third, so Mundinger was never able to resolve the issue."

One of his key achievements was the development of the two-year General Business program (later to become Business Management) and its numerous profiles.

"He recognized there were many niche areas for growth and that many students didn't want to spend three years in school.

Dean Eric Mundinger

He created a program that offered many options and met the needs of students and industry."

Another significant achievement was the development of Continuing Education. Mundinger believed that students who were unable to take a course during the day should be able to take the same course in the evening and achieve the same credit. Under his direction, day and evening courses were increasingly identical in content and quality – a concept that pleased both regular full-time students and those working on diplomas in the evening.

Mundinger worked hard to keep faculty spirits high. Communication was central to his management style, and he was known for his "state of the union" addresses at School social events. "He would tell faculty the direction the division was going within the College. He was good at letting us know where we were going and why," says Wheeler.

Eleanor Matthews agrees. As Mundinger's secretary, she was often central to his plans to show faculty and administration how much they were appreciated. For instance, back in the days when we all rushed to meet the same deadline for license renewal, Mundinger had Matthews stand in very long lineups in order to get license plate stickers for faculty and administration.

"We had a good group," she says. "Eric wanted everything done the right way but he also believed in boosting morale."

Mundinger's management style was a unique blend of the cutting edge and the traditional. On one hand, he was a proponent of a four-day workweek. On the other hand, he insisted all the men in the office dress in suits and ties.

"He believed his receptionist was the top person because everyone saw her first, that how they perceived us was influenced by what they saw at the front desk. And he was very particular about how we answered the phones."

Matthews tells us that Mundinger took a keen interest in Igor's Dining Room, the restaurant run by the School's Hotel and Restaurant program (which later became the Hospitality program). He often used it as a meeting place to impress representatives from industry. In fact, his office was so involved with the restaurant that Matthews spent part of her time straightening out menus and arranging reservations for College faculty.

Mundinger is also widely remembered as a sports enthusiast who established an annual golf tournament for faculty, students and industry. Many of those who took part in that event still smile at the mention of his name.

Perhaps the saddest note in the history of the Business School is the untimely death of Eric Mundinger. After being diagnosed with cancer, he continued to perform as dean from his hospital bed. In 1981, at the age of 43, he passed away.

John Liphardt became the next dean. In 1969, when John Almond asked him to join the faculty, Liphardt accepted because he was interested in the School's co-op programs. He rose quickly through the ranks, taking on positions as coordinator and chair before becoming dean.

"John Liphardt was broadly recognized as a decent, ethical and considerate gentleman. As a result, he was extraordinarily well respected," says Richard Hook, Vice President Academic.

Liphardt oversaw the School during a time of significant growth. During this period the School – through its efficiency – earned revenue that was used to support many other areas of the College. What's more, the School was commonly used as an example of a solidly-managed, efficient and effective academic unit.

"I got the School up to about 3,000 students," says Liphardt, who has since retired. "It increased quite significantly. At one point half of Humber's Continuing Education was business and we had, by far, the biggest day programs. While I was there we went from one chair to five. Humber had faith in me."

Dean John Liphardt

Like Mundinger, Liphardt was a strong supporter of Continuing Education. He continued along the path set out by his predecessor, ensuring that day and evening courses were integrated. He took it one step farther by setting up a dinner for day and evening staff to encourage networking and professional development.

"I believed that by attracting great people to teach in the evening you had a good network of contacts for full-time day teachers," says Liphardt.

Liphardt was an advocate of expanding ones' horizons. He encouraged his staff to continue their education and pursue other interests because he knew it all found its way back into the classroom.

And he practiced what he preached. He became the first dean to take advantage of the Masters of Education in Community Colleges program set up by Roy Giroux with Central Michigan University. The program allowed staff and faculty of Humber to take classes at the College.

To further develop himself – and complete his degree – Liphardt took a sabbatical.

"I told every faculty member to get renewed and refreshed, so I decided to do the same. My family and I lived in England for a year. While I was there I was able to interact with schools in England, Scotland and Germany. I got a sense of diverse educational systems and I also got in touch with European and international industries. It was a great experience."

A year after returning from England, the College experienced a reorganization and Liphardt became Principal of the Lakeshore campus, where he worked closely with Ken Simon and Michael Hatton. Seven years later, in the reorganization of 1994, he was made Dean of Computer Information Systems, Accounting and Computer Engineering and Electronics – a new school that combined programs that had been part of the Business School with programs from technology.

"As a result of having held three different dean roles, I understood more about the College," he says.

From 1985 to 1986, during Liphardt's sabbatical, Richard Hook acted as dean. "To signal the importance of learning and teaching (beyond the School's reputation for administrative efficiency), I asked the academic administrators to teach," says Hook, now Vice President Academic. "I taught marketing and enjoyed my link with the marketing faculty. I felt — and others may have different views — that teaching revitalized the administration's understanding of classroom and teaching issues and made us a more effective team. I think that it probably gave administration and faculty a better link."

"It was also an era in which the personal computer was just beginning to make new inroads into the business world. I can remember a long Legal Secretary Advisory Committee meeting in which staff and most advisors advocated for a new electric typewriter lab stating that 'Legal offices did not use word processors or computers for producing legal documents.'"

"After 45 minutes of debate, one solicitor in the committee finally agreed that his firm did use word processors to create documents and that there were no legal barriers to doing so. We finally agreed on desktop computers with word processing software, rather than electric typewriters or dedicated word processors. This was an important watershed for the School: prior to 85/86 the School had relied, for almost 20 years, entirely on the mainframe computer. This was our first move into personal computers."

Indeed, it was a very busy year. It was during Hook's tenure that the School introduced the first certificate program for university graduates: Human Resource Management.

"Don Wheeler was a strong advocate for this venture," says Hook. "This program supported a staggering rate of professionalization of the human resources field and anticipated, by a decade and a half, the current professional demand for degree entry to practice."

At the time, there was also a challenge in customer service.

"Generally, the staff and faculty were very considerate of students but the class scheduling process was lengthy, inefficient and frustrating for students. Lineups continued for several days into each semester while frustrated students waited to work out their timetable with a faculty adviser knowing that their options were slowly running out. While I cannot say that we made significant improvements in that year, the processes were dramatically enhanced during the next several years."

The dean who saw the greatest improvements in that area, then, was Jack Buckley. Buckley joined the Health Sciences division in 1970 as an administrator. He'd been very successful in developing new programs that significantly increased enrollment in full- and part-time programs, while increasing service in the health sector.

College administration saw Buckley's skills as transferable. In 1987, he was made Dean of the Business School, with a mandate to develop a series of postgraduate programs. As it turned out, that was just one of many areas Buckley influenced – not the least of which was the School's name.

"In the beginning it was known as the Business Division, but the title changed when I became dean and it became known as the School of Business."

"We were the first at the College. No other academic division was referred to as a School. We did it for a marketing advantage because it made the School comparable to other post-secondary institutions."

"We also did it to increase the profile within the College. At that time the Business School was a cash cow and was taken for granted. Enrollment had been slipping somewhat, which was important because the Business School's funding was crucial to the College as a whole."

"Also, we were housed in less than satisfactory accommodations," says Buckley. "The environment was such that there was no encouragement for faculty to remain on campus. I wanted to make faculty more accessible for students and create a business-like environment, but we were handicapped by a lack of funds."

"The other challenge was to rejuvenate the curriculum because every program at that time had changed very little from the beginning. The other concern was to ensure we met appropriate standards related to computer technology."

After identifying his challenges, Buckley went to work – and with great success. "We did increase enrollment and we built new offices. We also improved the curriculum and added some new programs as well."

In an attitude reminiscent of John Almond, Buckley emphasized currency and pushed faculty members to stay up to date with curriculum content. "I've been associated with community colleges for 30 years," he says. "One of my beliefs is this: the strength of the faculty rests on their expertise in the discipline they're teaching, and the currency of that expertise."

"The longer a person is on full-time faculty the more challenging that currency becomes. That's a constant concern for administration and faculty. I tried to provide opportunities for faculty to get practical experience that would augment the knowledge and skills they had at the time of hiring. We gave them opportunities to work in their own fields through activities like the exchange program with industry."

"One of the big advantages we had at the time was that many faculty carried on their own businesses in their fields of expertise."

In 1990, Buckley was given the chance to head up a new

Dean Jack Buckley

college in Nova Scotia. The task at hand was the amalgamation of 15 different colleges into one institution. Since he is originally from Nova Scotia, he couldn't resist the opportunity. "I look back very fondly on my days at Humber," he says. "If that presidency hadn't opened up I'd have retired there."

Upon Buckley's departure, a competition was held to replace him. This time, there was a focus on business experience. Lloyd Rintoul was the successful candidate, beating out several internal applicants. As everyone will agree, Rintoul attacked the position with gusto.

"Lloyd Rintoul was Humber's second dean selected from the private sector," says Richard Hook. "Lloyd's interest in international markets, customer service and quality management were important features of his term of office."

"He worked to open markets for Humber in Southeast Asia, Germany and Mexico and was a strong supporter of, and advocate for, College development initiatives in these areas. He was an active student of marketing and customer service literature and looked to apply new concepts being developed by academics and implemented in the private sector."

Rintoul was passionate about Total Quality Management (TQM), a popular management system of the day that called for revising and enhancing processes within a quality paradigm.

"His enthusiasm for TQM was reflected in his efforts to apply an industry model of TQM to the Business School," says Hook.

"With the support of a number of faculty and administrators, a thoughtfully integrated process was implemented. But like all imported systems, TQM had its limitations. Some of these limitations related to the fact that the concept was foreign to the College and decisions proposed by the quality councils were not always easily resourced. Also, while the measurement processes offered by the TQM literature were useful in enhancing decision making, some felt that the terminology and expectations were more relevant to manufacturing and production. It was seen by many staff as a 'foreign' concept and did not take off at Humber."

"The Business School TQM experiment reminded the College that 'change management' required more than a concept that had worked well in another setting," says Hook. "Lloyd and I frequently reflected on TQM progress and tended to agree that continuous improvement was a far more acceptable strategy for Humber than the more structured industry approach to TQM. In fact, based upon our learning, Humber's Institutional Research Office has evolved as an arm to provide information to staff teams for the purpose of encouraging improvements. Indeed, data-driven continuous change is the essence of continuous improvement."

Rintoul left in 1994, leaving the Business School in the hands of the Chairs. The "Dean in a Team," as they called themselves, managed the School until the reorganization later that year. Afterward, the School was in the hands of Chairs John Riccio and Toby Fletcher. For a brief period, when Riccio went on sick leave, Vice President Richard Hook filled in.

Associate Dean Toby Fletcher

It wasn't until 1997 that the Business School had its next dean. After a long search, an internal candidate was selected. Michael Hatton, who had been Dean of Media Studies, was appointed to the position. Under his leadership, the Lakeshore and North campuses were finally united, the North Campus Business School offices were expanded and renovated to include most staff and faculty, and the School made its first foray into degree-level education. Plus, the name was changed to the "Business School at Humber College" to be even more closely identified with the country's most successful business schools, which used similar monikers.

Associate Dean John Riccio

And enrollment increased dramatically.

"First of all, a curriculum review of our flagship programs that took place in 1998 positioned them better in the marketplace," says Dean Hatton, explaining the growth in student numbers. "Secondly, we have actively worked at having higher entry standards for getting into those programs than other colleges in the GTA and the province. Consequently, we've developed a reputation for being the school that's a little tougher to get into and that has resulted in stronger students and almost certainly a lower attrition rate. That, in turn, brings more resources to Humber and the Business School."

"The third element is our marketing focus and within that our promotional campaigns. The magazine we publish is unique, and that has helped us develop a very specific relationship with guidance counselors who call and ask for class sets," says Dean Hatton about *Connections*, a magazine published annually by the School.

Marketing has evolved in the six years that Hatton has been dean. The most recent campaign – "Seating is Limited" – continues to emphasize the exclusivity of Business School programs. "We began with creating new fact sheets on every program, then we developed short program brochures and our most recent overall campaign 'Seating is Limited.' The message is that not everyone can get in. You'll have to be a little better, apply a little earlier, and be a little stronger. We believe we are the target for the strongest business-bound students in Canada. No other business schools in the country market their programs as we do. We've issued a series of school-based posters whereas other colleges are satisfied with college-based brochures."

"And now we're starting program-based brochures. The new Law Clerk program and the Court and Tribunal Agent program have their posters – and so does Professional Golf Management."

Hatton believes that marketing is pointless unless you have the product to back it up. With that in mind, he devotes a great deal of thought to program offerings.

"I would say we currently offer four types of programs in the Business School. We have a large intake in the Business Administration and Business Management diploma programs, programs that are offered by virtually all colleges and some universities. Then we have a series of niche-oriented programs, such as Financial Services, Law Clerk, Court and Tribunal Agent and Golf. We also have a series of postgraduate programs. In fact, we have more postgraduate programs and higher enrollment in them than any other school in the province and likely the rest

of Canada. Several of our postgraduate programs and our niche programs are unique in the country, like the International Project Management program. Finally, we now have new four-year degree level programs."

"We understand what our product groupings are and we differentiate ourselves on that basis. We market the School and we market the programs," says Dean Hatton. "And as we do, enrollment continues to grow."

Like the deans before him, he's having an impact. His passion is helping form the School's character, as did John Almond, Eric Mundinger, John Liphardt, Richard Hook, Jack Buckley, and Lloyd Rintoul.

Together their accomplishments are the stepping stones upon which the Business School advances to meet the challenges of the future.

Dean Michael J. Hatton

Index

Presidents, Deans, Associate Deans

Faculty and others

Programs

Other

Campuses/Schools

Business School alumni with Dean Mundinger and President Wragg, 1979 (bottom row, centre)